ALLIANCE, ILLINOIS

ALLIANCE, ILLINOIS

DAVE ETTER

Northwestern University Press
Evanston, Illinois

Northwestern University Press
Evanston, Illinois 60208-4170

Printed in the United States of America

10 9 8 7 6 5 4 3 2 1

ISBN 0-8101-2213-8

Library of Congress Cataloging-in-Publication data are available from the
Library of Congress.

The paper used in this publication meets the minimum requirements of the
American National Standard for Information Sciences–Permanence of Paper for
Printed Library Materials, ANSI Z39.48-1992.

To Peggy, Emily, and George,
and to everyone who has shared my Illinois years

A windmill, a junk heap, and a Rotarian in their American setting have more meaning to me than Notre Dame, the Parthenon, or the heroes of the ages. I understand them. I get them emotionally.
— Thomas Hart Benton

But I'm interested primarily in people, in man in conflict with himself, with his fellow man, or with his time and place, his environment.
— William Faulkner

...there is nothing more native than speech.
— George Ade

There always was a relationship between poet and place. Placeless poetry, existing in the non-geography of ideas, is a modern invention and not a very fortunate one.
— Archibald MacLeish

In the end a man can expect to understand no land but his own.
— Vachel Lindsay

Just this: we are "West of Chicago," and that's like being "East of Suez." It makes a difference.
— Richard Bissell

CONTENTS

ACKNOWLEDGMENTS

Most of these poems have appeared in *Alliance, Illinois* (Kylix Press), *Cornfields* (Spoon River Poetry Press), and *West of Chicago* (Spoon River Poetry Press). Several poems have appeared in *Crabtree's Woman* (BkMk Press), *Bright Mississippi* (Juniper Press), *Central Standard Time* (BkMk Press), *Open to the Wind* (Uzzano Press), *Riding the Rock Island Through Kansas* (Wolfsong), and *Voyages to the Inland Sea* (University of Wisconsin — La Crosse).

Poems in this volume have also appeared in the following publications: *Abraxas, Ann Arbor Review, Applecart, Ark River Review, Back Door, The Chariton Review, Chicago Review, Chicago Tribune Magazine, Chouteau Review, The Chowder Review, Cincinnati Poetry Review, Colorado State Review, Cottonwood Review, Cream City Review, Cutbank, Dacotah Territory, December, The Dragonfly, Epos, The Far Point, Focus/Midwest, The Great Lakes Review, The Greenfield Review, The Harrison Street Review, Hearse, Hiram Poetry Review, Icarus, Illinois Quarterly, Images, The Kansas City Star, Kansas Quarterly, The Lake Superior Review, Long Pond Review, The Madison Review, Midwest, Midwest Poetry Review, The Midwest Quarterly, The Minnesota Review, The Nation, Nebraska Review, New: American and Canadian Poetry, New Letters, The New Moon, New Tomorrow, New Work/s* (Duck Down Press), *The North American Review, Northeast, Northern Lights, The North Stone Review, Oakwood, Open Places, Pebble, Peninsula Review, Poetry Northwest, Poetry Now, Practices of the Wind, Prairie Schooner, Quartet, Raccoon, Rain, Rapport, River Bottom, The Salt Creek Reader, Salt Lick, Shenandoah, South Dakota Review, South Florida Poetry Journal, Sou'wester, The Spoon River Quarterly, Stinktree, Stuffed Crocodile, Sumac, Tennessee Poetry Journal, Three Rivers Poetry Journal, Today, TriQuarterly, Uzzano, Wells Elevator, Wind,* and *Wisconsin Review.*

"Body," "Homework," "Jane's Blue Jeans," "Living in the Middle," "Moonlight Yodel," and "Public Library" first appeared in *Poetry.*

GEORGE MAXWELL:
County Seat

Pushing deep into Sunflower County now,
just minutes before sunup,
the big semitrailer truck droning on
in the breezy, dew-heavy darkness;
leaving behind the cornfields,
the red barns, the windbreak trees,
snorting by the city limits sign
announcing ALLIANCE, pop. 6,428,
thumping across the railroad tracks
of the Chicago and North Western,
slipping past roadside produce stands
and hamburger and milkshake drive-ins,
bouncing and rattling again
between the bruised bodies of billboards
saying where to shop, eat, sleep,
where to fill up with gas:
LICHENWALNER'S DEPARTMENT STORE,
CARL'S MAINLINE CAFE,
HOTEL TALL CORN,
BOB'S TEXACO;
dipping toward the polluted waters
of the sluggish Ausagaunaskee River
and the once stately section of town
where neglected Victorian houses,
with their cupolas and wide porches,
are set back on maple-shaded lawns;
remembering good and bad times,
lost faces, half-forgotten names;
and then the driver taking a last drag
from his Marlboro cigarette,
poking me in the ribs
with yellow, tobacco-stained fingers,
one letter of Jesus on each knuckle,

1

breaking the long silence between us
by saying over the asthmatic breathing
of the great diesel engine
that we are here, this is it,
here's that town you've been asking for;
moving slowly into the Square,
with its domed and clocked courthouse,
its bandstand and Civil War monument,
its two-story brick buildings,
lawyers and doctors above,
the town's merchants below;
stopping on Main Street
next to the Farmers National Bank,
stepping down to the curb,
thanking the driver for the lift,
grabbing a U.S. Army duffel bag,
slamming the cab door with a loud bang,
then turning around to face
ALLIANCE CHAMBER OF COMMERCE
WELCOMES YOU
TO THE HYBRID CORN CAPITAL OF AMERICA,
and thus knowing for dead certain
that I'm back in the hometown,
and that nothing has, nothing could have
really changed since I went away.

CHESTER GREENE:
Taking the Census

Vines hold up the webby porch.
The birdbath hoards a dune of sand.
Broken toys bleed along a sagging fence.
But around in back
a Maytag washing machine
hums like a hive
and shirts are strung on a frayed line
that disappears in leaves.
I sit on the broken springs of an old car seat
and ask the usual questions.
Mrs. O'Toole folds red hands
over a watermelon belly
and tells me that nine sons are not enough.
I look about in horror.
The baby gives me a choice of worms.
I choose the one hanging out of his mouth.
Four boys are Indians.
They glare from their private tree.
The other four are cowboys.
None of them wear white hats.
The biggest boy asks me to join their game.
When I turn the invitation down flat,
an arrow gets me
right between the eyes.
I surrender quickly to both sides.
The gun barrel hurts my ribs.
Now, Mrs. O'Toole lies in the dust.
The cowboys have long ropes.
The redskins bring the fire.

AMANDA PURTILL:
Four Rows of Sweet Corn

It's strange you should tell me
he's not coming today
to turn the earth in the side yard,
when just an hour or so ago
he said, "I'll be there at ten,
or if not then, then later on,
say, four or five this afternoon."
No, I can't figure him out.
Maybe he's still smarting at something
I said last time he was here,
something about his daydreaming,
gazing off, staring at the blowing trees.
He's touchy, there's no denying that.
He told me the world would keep
whether I grew food or not.
Nevertheless, summer won't be much
of a summer season to me
if I can't watch some squash growing,
and beans and tomatoes,
and my four rows of sweet corn.

HENRY LICHENWALNER:
Living in the Middle

Here in Alliance, Illinois,
I'm living in the middle,
standing on the Courthouse lawn
in the middle of town,
in the middle of my life,
a self-confessed middlebrow,
a member of the middle class,
and of course Middle Western,
the middle, you see, the middle,
believing in the middle way,
standing here at midday
in the middle of the year,
breathing the farm-fragrant air
of Sunflower County,
in the true-blue middle
of middle America,
in the middle of my dreams.

MITCH VALENTINE:
Billboard

The billboard is just plain tacky.
A hometown disgrace is what it is.
But as I stare at it today
from the weeds across the street,
a workman in bib overalls
finally gets a new bill in place.
Hooray, a circus is coming,
coming here to Sunflower County!
"We'll be there," I say to Prince,
who lifts his head and barks sharply.
Then we run home together,
down sun-dappled brick sidewalks,
so anxious to spread the news
to the other neighborhood dogs:
Lucas, Lion, Lobo and Max.

TANYA OWENS:
Equality

They don't brag about me much
in Sunflower County.
But they love me
and they cheer me real good
all over the Middle West.
And I mean places
like Toledo,
Sioux Falls, St. Louis,
Peoria, Waterloo,
Kansas City, St. Paul,
Omaha, Fort Wayne,
Chicago, Milwaukee,
all them big towns
you probably heard about
from picture postcards.
There are no write-ups about me
in the local papers.
But when I step into the ring
to wrestle some girl
from Sheboygan or someplace
and the announcer says
to the crowd in the arena,
"In this corner,
from Alliance, Illinois,
weighing 196 pounds,
Tanya Owens,"
I know I'm somebody special
and flex my new muscles.
Patrick talks me up proud.
He's some sweet husband,
that good boy is.
You won't find no loose
anti-women's-lib talk
hanging from his lips.
"We're equals," he tells them
at Jim's barbershop.
"We both weigh 196 pounds."

REX AGEE:
Getting at the Truth

"There's more honest information
in a tomato can label
than in a week of newspapers,"
said Sherwood Anderson. So I
canceled the *Tribune,* the *Gazette,*
and the *Chronicle* and spent the
money on canned tomatoes. Then,
as the years skipped by, I forgot
about the *Tribune,* the *Gazette,*
and the *Chronicle.* My friends said
they were informed that I was the
smartest tomato can reader
in the entire Middle West. And
they never picked that news up from
any old newspaper, either.

VALERIE MAYHEW:
Cornfield Virgin

It was bad enough of you, Otis Riley,
to make that ruckus on the porch,
to swear and smash my new geranium pot
when I told you, "No, no, no,
you can't do that, no, never that."
But to stand there and repeat
over and over and over and over again
in that singsong voice of yours,
"Valerie Mayhew is a cornfield virgin,
Valerie Mayhew is a cornfield virgin,"
was the limit, the very limit.
The front room was loud with male talk,
thick with weather, politics, and crops,
so I think none of the men heard you.
But the kitchen window was open,
and my married aunts and pregnant cousins
who were drying supper dishes heard.
They heard. They heard it all.
Later, Mother, high on dandelion wine,
barged into the upstairs bathroom,
where I was soaking in a hot tub,
and said, in a blunt, loose-tongue way,
"Who's a virgin? Who's a virgin?
There's no son or daughter of mine
who's not been to the hayloft
at least once under the spell
of a spring moon or harvest itch."
So you've gone and done it, Otis.
Now when I talk about the wild boys
I went to college with down in Macomb,
the ones I parked in the weeds with,
they'll smile and their eyes will say,
"You're just a cornfield virgin, Val."

OLIVER BRIGGS:
Night Work

He got out of the car.
Got out his driver's license.
He said "yes, sir,
no, sir, yes, sir."
He was polite as hell.
He was polite as hell.
He was polite as hell.
Then his girl friend
moves up to the car window
and shoots me in the shoulder.
A .38 Smith and Wesson.
Pulled it from her handbag.
"Take that, copper," she says.
Called me "copper."
Right out of a thirties movie.
"Take that, copper."
I went down of course.
Of course I went down.
Then he got back in the car
and they drove away.
Not burning rubber, not fast.
Like they had all night.
He was polite as hell.
He said "yes, sir,
no, sir, yes, sir."
Jesus, this night work
is going to kill me yet.

WADE HOLLENBACH:
Hard Cider

"Can I come too?" she said.
I said nothing and kept on walking,
moving away quickly down the railroad track.
But one-eyed Billie June came,
and she grabbed my hand and grinned.
Near the bridge we stopped and looked
at the moonlit waters
of the Ausagaunaskee River.
For a minute, I forgot she was with me,
lost as I was in my faraway thoughts,
my troubles in finding a new job.
"What's in the sack?" she said.
I pulled out the tall dusty bottle.
"Hard cider?" she said.
"Hard cider," I said.
I screwed off the cap and took a long swallow.
"Can I have some?" she said.
I passed her the bottle.
She helped herself to three big gulps.
Her teeth were yellow, her dress was soiled,
and a hunk of coal-black hair
had fallen over her one good eye.
"Hard cider!" she said.
"Take it easy," I said,
"we've got a whole night ahead of us."
She kissed me smack on the lips,
knocking off my hat, dropping the bottle.
"Hard cider," I said,
and hurled a stone into the river.

SUSAN COBB:
Names

I want to be Susan Jonquil,
a bold springtime flower
sticking out of a jelly glass.
Or Susan Ferris Wheel.
Or Susan Television,
my bare tummy warm with loud pictures.
Or Susan Blueberry Muffin.
Or Susan Iuka, an Indian girl
sparkling in beads and silver rings.
But more than anything,
I want to be Susan Mississippi,
a river that does what it wants to,
and anytime it wants to,
moving south past fish and funny boats,
past moonlit towns and hooting owls.
And Susan Honeysuckle
would be summers of fun.
And so would Susan Lemonade
and Susan Lawnmower.
Look, I'm telling you right now,
being plain Susan Cobb
is no great thrill to me.

TUCKER STONE:
Stuttering Hands

The broken-down barn of a man,
his face an Appalachia of ruts and gullies,
leans against the weathered bricks
of the Farmers National Bank.

It has quit raining again.
The high school boys coming up Main Street
break into a runaway gallop.
They are wild horses drunk in a green wind.

Approaching forty, I realize
that I am really terrified of growing old.
Already the buxom farm girls
are aware of my stuttering hands.

ROGER POWELL:
The Talk at Rukenbrod's

I sit in the shade on the high curb
in front of Rukenbrod's grocery store.
I sip a cold Nehi Grape and listen to the talk:

"You remember Andy Gump, don't you?"

"My blue jeans are too tight, she tells me.
I feel creepy walking past the Square
with all those dirty eyes scraping my skin."

"No, I never knew Nettles. He was an Elk."

"Sure, Paul was farming in Pickaway County, Ohio,
but he got going in this spiritualism stuff.
Goes all over now, West Coast and all."

"Butterflies, you know, taste with their feet."

"The wife took the kids down to Hannibal,
Mark Twain's hometown on the Mississippi.
I told her to bring me back a nice souvenir."

"Joe Palooka I remember. My brother Jake liked him."

"Nettles ran a forklift up at the cannery.
Then he was with A&W Root Beer, nights.
Heart attack it was. In Terre Haute, I heard."

"A purple martin eats 2,000 insects per day."

"So I think I got me a modest daughter, see.
But last week I catch her with another girl.
And they weren't playing no dominoes, neither."

"Fred's cousin was formerly with Dial-a-Prayer."

"Guess what they brought me from Hannibal?
A Becky Thatcher back scratcher! No lie.
I didn't know whether to laugh or throw a fit."

"Butterflies do what? Taste with their what?"

I take my empty into Rukenbrod's grocery store.
They have run out of Nehi Grape.
I grab a Dr. Pepper and sit down again.

"You sure you don't remember Andy Gump?"

FLORA RUTHERFORD:
Postcard to Florida

What brightens up this prairie town in spring?
Not tulip, not dandelion, not willow leaf,
but New Holland, Massey-Ferguson, and John Deere.
Right, the brand-new farm equipment
glistening now in the rooster-strutting sun.
And oh what colors they have given us:
strawberry red, sweet-corn yellow, pie-apple green.
A fragrant breeze drifts in from the plowed earth.
The excitement of crops seeds my furrowed brain.
Mother, we have come through another wintertime,
and I had to write and tell you this.

ORVILLE JUMP:
Me, Myself, and I

The thin boy came out of the tall cornfield.
He had on blue jeans and a jean jacket.
I stared hard at his adolescent face.
Damn, this was me thirty-five years ago.
The same sandy hair, the same gray-green eyes.
But there were smears of blood on his right hand,
and his left hand held a bloody rabbit.
"Some animal got to him first," he said,
"and I finished him off with my jackknife."
A cold wind rustled the ragged cornstalks.
No, this wasn't me, this was never me.
Then I recalled the bird I stabbed to death,
the bluejay the cat caught when I was twelve.
"Bastard," I said, and punched him where he smiled.

STANLEY ADAMS:
County Road K

I said: "Slow down. Good lord, man, this road
ain't no interstate highway, you know.
Look at the damn dust you're raisin' up."

He said: "So what. The gravel and junk
shoots behind us. We're not gettin' none.
I always drive fast, no matter what."

I said: "Sure thing. But if one big stone
jumps up and cracks a headlight, you'll quit.
You just ain't usin' no common sense."

He said: "Shit, Stan. No need to sweat blood.
We hit blacktop again past that farm.
Sit back, stay cool, and enjoy the view."

CLARENCE FOWLER:
Nuts and Bolts

Now what's a *Farm Journal* doing in a doctor's office?

Look, if I could only point to a tractor
out in someone's cornfield or in the barnyard
and announce with an authoritative voice,
Say, there's a Massey-Ferguson 1130:
Perkins direct-injection diesel engine,
turbocharged 120 horsepower,
hydrostatic power-steering,
air conditioned cab, air-luxe seat, etcetera,
it just might make my mechanically-minded son
sit up and take another glance at his old man.

Think hard: Do I know a nut from a bolt?

And then if I could go on to proclaim,
ever so casually, you understand,
Hey, take a gander, will you, at the brand-new
New Holland 1469 haybine mower-conditioner:
37 horses, water-cooled engine,
and a sickle bar that can cut hay
at 1,520 strokes per minute,
the boy might even forgive me somewhat
for being Sunflower County's leading seller
of women's dresses and women's hats and shoes.

Should I study up? Is it too late to learn the score?

BRUCE PUTNAM:
Crayola

It was just a child's
crayon drawing,
but perfect somehow:
broad blue prairies
soaking in mist,
a lightning tree
still supporting
a rope swing,
and in the foreground
a bushy dog
asleep on a hill
of sycamore leaves.

''And where am I
in your picture?''
I asked her,
tugging a yellow braid.
''Oh, you're not here,''
she said, sadly.
''You've gone away
to Cincinnati,
dreaming of me
lost in a brick town
with too many weeds
and fences.''

MELISSA JENKINS:
Staring Into Winter

Big flakes of snow
fall on the last remaining oak tree leaves.
I love the dry, ticking sound they make
on this storm threatening afternoon.
There should be an owl somewhere nearby,
tightening his feathers and staring into winter.
I know there are deer about,
for I have seen two of them cross the road
day before yesterday,
just up past the railroad tracks.
And where is the red fox
that jumped the barbed wire last spring,
hightailing it out of Ruby Cooper's chicken yard?
Snow in big flakes
thickens in the scrap of oak woods on the hill.
I have an empty house to go to
and cold thoughts to rattle in my head.
Pray for me, Father,
and for the deer whose gentle eyes
are the color of syrup bubbling in the pan.

JAMIE MCFEE:
Big Sister

Patty's legs, the bruises a deep purple,
were hanging out of the windy tree.
I wanted to talk to her face
but it was hidden in the dancing leaves.
This was the time of her first trouble,
her walking around seeing none of us,
even falling down the cellar stairs.
Now she was up there in the carved maple
sucking hard on something juicy.
I didn't know what it was, but juice drips
would come down wetting my hot cheeks.
My neck was beginning to cramp a bit,
with my head poked up that way,
looking into the sister-hiding tree.
I couldn't get up there, couldn't make
that first big branch to swing a leg over,
though I had tried and tried hard,
wanting to keep up with her if I could.
I had my radio on the music
and it was twanging in my good ear.
Patty was still eating something runny
and yelled for me to turn down the sound.
"You know that song makes me sad," she said.
She was always, always saying that,
even crying suddenly at supper table,
remembering what was unhappy someplace.
I slid around the tree trunk a little,
hoping to get a better look at her.
The music was banging in my skull,
wilder than wild rain or tornado winds,
a dozen overheated guitars going crazy.
Then a strong breeze came swooshing in,
and her dress blew up with the leaves.
There was a blood-red spot on her panties,
and maybe this was part of her trouble.

My neck was hurting more and my back too.
It was no fun standing there,
seeing purple legs but not Patty's face,
and she not caring to play a game
or ride bikes or roll on the grass,
though I asked her to and begged her to.
So I turned up the radio on the music
until it was as loud as it would go,
and walked through the flower beds,
kicking at all the blood-red tulip faces,
wondering if it was a good thing
to grow up and be grown up
and not like anything anymore.

YVONNE WYNCOOP:
Looking at Clouds

I am looking at black rain clouds
and a patch of bright blue sky
the exact shape of Illinois,
a state where my crazy aunt Minnie
spent her whole life saying,
"Aren't we ever going to move from here?"
Look, the patch of sky is looking
very much now like Delaware,
a state my aunt never heard of.
And a good thing, too, since that's
a place she would have raved about,
what with all those historic houses
and first families with family trees
rooted among the dank bogs of England.
No, she would have never shut up
had she known about Delaware
and the thin green mists they have there,
her bony finger tracing the map
eastward out of Sunflower County.

FRANK TEMPLE:
Wet Spring, Dark Earth

Hope

Wasting away in her bed of psalms,
my mother opens tired eyes to say,
"I'll be on my feet in a week or two."

Agony

She will have no doctors, no drugs.
The Lord is her shepherd, her trust.
But His rod, His staff don't comfort me.

Death

Here on April's tulip-trembling hill
the gravestones darken in the thin rain.
We stop at a fresh grave, a new stone.

Love

Sister Betsy, seven years old in May,
shows me her buggy of sleeping dolls.
"Every one of them is a mama," she says.

Memory

My father stands under a fragile moon,
pounding cold fist into cold hand,
his Donna dying in a gospeled room.

Faith

Deep in a green-bladed field of corn
I pray I may honor my mother's faith,
and know that in God there is no death.

MOLLY DUNAWAY:
Rainbow

When I get good and mad at my man
I take off my engagement ring
and put it in the empty Rainbo bread wrapper
that I keep under the bed
or slung away on a top closet shelf.
Red and blue and oodles of yellow:
such a happy wrapper to wrap bread in,
but much too gay and giddy
for an off again on again diamond ring.
Then I'll watch a mushy movie on TV
and get choked up at the love scenes
and run upstairs and get out my ring,
safe and secure in its bread wrapper.
Today it rained, and we had a rainbow,
all candy pink and watery gold.
I didn't wear my man's ring all day.
Rainbo bread, slices of the well-fed dream.
My bright dreams of love, of loving him:
are they real as Rainbo bread?
or only fast-fading rainbow dreams?

NEIL CAMPBELL:
Humor

My long-time buddy Humpy Walls,
a hunchback who writes the sports news
for our own *Alliance Gazette,*
has a priceless sense of humor.
Take this afternoon, for instance.
We're coming out of the Elite,
after cherry pie and coffee,
when we bump into Bert Foster,
who works at Guthrie's Feed and Grain,
and who says, his face close to Hump's,
"Hey, Walls, it's been damn near two years.
Where's the seven bucks you owe me?"
Humpy just grins his grin, then says,
"Don't you worry, Bert, you'll get it
when I get myself straightened up."

ZACHARY GRANT:
Guilt

We drive to Chicago's Union Station.
I say goodbye, give her a quick kiss.
My Nancy Lee is going off to New Hampshire.
We never got along. I'm glad she's gone.
But then, back home again, it hits me:
I saw only her faults, her blemishes.
After brooding over a few whiskey sours,
I stumble around in a blues funk.
The neighbors put away their porch swing.
A truck dumps coal at the fuel company.
Sad and alone in October's smoky twilight,
I walk through the black walnut trees.
Across the broken limestone wall, I see
rusty soup cans, a discarded water heater.
A squirrel scampers among dry leaves.
The empty birdhouse darkens on its pole.
Far off, a freight train blows for a crossing.
The wind turns cold. I think of snow.
Well, there's not much more I can say.
I was always right. Now I'm wrong.
I know it's no picnic being a father,
but if you have an ugly-duckling daughter,
close your eyes and love her to death.

STUBBY PAYNE:
Stocking Tops

In June the syringa bushes bloom,
and I swear that I can smell oranges there.
That was your smell, Bee. I knew it well.

And I think of you today in Arne's Pub,
where all winter long you sipped Gordon's gin,
legs crossed, showing a bulge of creamy thigh
above those tantalizing stocking tops.

Green summer again. Rain. The warm earth steams.

You left town on a Burlington day coach
to visit an aunt in Prairie du Chien.
"She's full of money," you said, "and dying of cancer."

Toward the end of July,
Sunflower County cornfields turn blond.
Stiff tassels shake in the sexual sun.
There's a dust of pollen in the air.

How many bags of potato chips?
How many trips to the can?
Oh, how many quarters in the jukebox, Bee?

August heat. The girls go almost naked here.

Like some overworked Cinderella,
you always took off just before midnight
on the arm of Prince or Joe or Hal or Smith,
bound for your place above the shoe store.

Yes, I should have bedded down with you myself,
said so what if you were a bumbling barfly,
every drinking man's little honey bush.

AMOS BLACKBURN:
War of the Hybrids

Who has conquered these Midwestern cornfields?

Pioneer
Northrup King
Stewart
Dairyland
Pride
Lynks
DeKalb
Cargill
O's Gold
Acco
Funk's G-Hybrid
Hughes
Jacques
P-A-G
McNair
Trojan
Big D
Super Crost
Hulting
Bo-Jac

See their proud signs in the September sun.

PRUDENCE ARCHER:
Thirteen

There are girl dreams I can make out of snow,
always using this house in snowfall December,
a wedding cake house with pretty me in a snow-white dress,
ready to descend the staircase and disappear in snow,
off to the snowy Episcopal church and my wedding day.

These snow-cloud dreams of marriage vows and bridal cakes
have been going on for many snowball winters,
although I'm just thirteen and my snow-hating sisters
were married not in snow but in May, June, and September.

I'm Prudence Archer and I believe in snow.

KYLE TROWBRIDGE:
Bird's-Eye View

No, Ken's not the adventuresome kind.
When I told him there was a great view
of the western half of Prairie Street
from the top of his very own pine tree
and that he sure ought to make the trip
as it was damn well worth all the sweat,
he informed me in no uncertain words:
"Why climb up there just to look at
some more of what is right down here?"
"It's different, so different," I said.
"The tops of roofs, the spread of yards.
What you see is what a bird can see."
Then I climbed back up the tall pine
and called down the news that Amy Scott
was sunbathing with her halter off.
He frowned, and I knew it was no use
to talk to one so alive yet so dead.
"Big deal," he said, and closed his eyes.

NINA JAMES:
Writing Down the Dream

Courthouse clock bonging in my window.
Bedroom shaped like a loaf of french bread.
On the floor, red lace panties, red lace bra.
Thin blue shaft of frosty moonlight.
Walking out of the house with nothing on.
V of geese flying over packing plant.
Trolley car stops and I ride to cornfields.
Li'l Abner sipping a brown bottle of 3.2 beer.
Horse thief hanging from a horse barn hook.
My breasts swinging when I ran away.
Loud litanies and booming burial psalms.
Pioneers rising from pioneer graves.
Then I'm up in a tall cedar tree.
I'm eating penny candy, my jawbreaker going white.
Papa calling, "Get down, get down at once."
Pulls me by the ear into steamy kitchen.
Mama in saddle shoes frying eggs and bacon.
Zenith radio playing big band songs.
"Green Eyes," "One Dozen Roses," "Elmer's Tune."
Pink paper moon at our graduation dance.
Glenn Miller waving a golden trombone.
Now I'm at an afternoon double-feature movie.
Newsreel is full of soldiers and DC-3s.
Bombs falling on England, London on fire.
Returning home past a four-silo farm.
Bales of straw stacked against frame house.
Split-rail fence around an abandoned church.
Scarecrow, head resting on a hymnal.
Old Plank Road and Old Plank Bridge.
Something bulky down there in the river.
Body of biology teacher with snakes for hair.
Suddenly it grows dark, super dark.
Glare of steam locomotive's one-eyed stare.
I screamed, I screamed, didn't I?

LESTER RASMUSSEN:
Jane's Blue Jeans

Hanging alone on a blue-rain clothesline,
hanging alone in a blue rain,
hanging alone:

a pair of torn blue jeans,
a pair of faded blue jeans,
a pair of Jane's blue jeans.

Blue jeans in the shape of Jane,
Jane now in another pair of blue jeans,
blue jeans that also take the shape of Jane.

Oh, Jane, my rainy blues blue-jeans girl,
blue jeans without you inside
is the saddest blue I've seen all day.

WILL GOODENOW:
The Red Depot

Morning fog engulfs the red depot.
I move up closer and smell coal smoke.
There are phantoms on the brick platform,
ghosts that rode a lot of varnish.
Sherwood Anderson paces in his floppy felt hat.
Vachel Lindsay scribbles on an old envelope.
Carl Sandburg puffs a stub cigar.
Can I believe this? Can I?
Suddenly very excited, I take a look around.
A baggage wagon is loaded with sacks of mail.
Eight bankers check giant gold watches.
The stationmaster sells a ticket to Topeka.
Beyond the water tower a whistle wails.
Blue rails begin to hum.
Hey, that's it, that's the good music.
Eagerly, expectantly, I stare down the tracks.
The Corn Belt Limited will be right on time.
But I wait and wait and still no train comes.
Something's wrong. Something is terribly wrong.
Now the sun sucks the fog away.
I am standing in a new parking lot.
The red depot is a long-lost memory.
All the steam locomotives are gone to scrap.
Most of the engineers and firemen are dead.
No one's there to holler ''Allllll aboard!''

MICHAEL FLANAGAN:
Unemployed

In this tall frame house
with a turret and a weather vane,
I, Michael Flanagan,
a lumpy, round-shouldered guy
who too closely resembles
a sack of grain broken open,
sit at my rolltop desk
and draw tiny Ferris wheels
on a Trailways timetable.
Between window and bookcase
are my signed and sealed diplomas.
How does that old saying go:
"Never criticize the trapper
with the skins on the wall"?
Maybe so, but I still want a job.
There is no fun in living
second or third class.
I remember prim, blue-haired ladies
in a dumpy Wisconsin tavern
near the Soo Line tracks
drinking Potosi beer
and saying to each other,
"This is better than the Ritz"
and "It's great to slum it."
And a millhand turned to
a crane operator and said,
"What's this world coming to?"
An open book is what I want chiseled
on my marble gravestone,
and these simple words,
He never got off the bus.
Coming from a place so small

that the tallest building
was an Arco station,
I should have been prepared
to hear advice for the unemployed,
such as the mailman's,
"Perhaps you can catch on
at the car wash across town."
I gaze at the sheepskins
tacked neatly to the wall
and slump in my chair.
I am an empty burlap bag now,
the loose grain of my body
falling on the bare floorboards,
my tired, feeble thoughts turning
to carnival lights blowing
in the big Midwestern wind,
my father coming out
of the beer tent again,
his Irish-American face
red as a brakeman's flag.

DREW MANNING:
Harvest Dust

The carnival rays of the sun
illuminated the dust clouds
that rose behind a blue combine
harvesting forty-two acres
of good Illinois soybeans.
I stood there quietly,
the evening breeze around my head,
watching the dust thicken,
seeing emeralds and red tapestries,
seeing golden showers of rain.
Then the sun dropped behind
the last stretch of prairie,
and once again the dust
became no more than dust
in the cool and farm-dark air.

ABIGAIL TAYLOR:
Senility

At the city dump we saw
a bathtub with three feet.

Frank James made me black tea.
There are no lilies in our valley.
Nothing but lies about that man.
I want violets for my hair.

At the city dump we saw
a broom with two straws.

I did too know him, I did so too.
And that's why I spoke to him.
I knew him in Keokuk, Iowa.
And that's why he spoke to me.

At the city dump we saw
a stool with one leg.

The boy who loves me has a knife.
This is a funny place to stop.
Those birds are angry at me again.
I'll run away when I have to.

At the city dump we saw
a rag doll with no face.

WAT NUGENT:
Epitaph

I was born a bastard in a pickup truck
between two corn towns south of here
and wrapped in a sack the dog peed on.

I was always puny for my age,
never fast in school or first at sports,
quick to get lost and muddy.

I was born for cold, windy fields,
long hours behind the barn,
and machinery that wouldn't work.

I was dropped on my head at two,
crippled by a horse at twelve,
shot by a cracked duck hunter at twenty.

I was born to die piece by piece
and looked to death for a better life,
for life not death was the death of me.

ISAIAH ROODHOUSE:
Putting Off the Encyclopedia Salesman

No, the wife is not at home just now.
Well, actually, she's home,
but she's back in our corn patch
picking out some ripe ones for supper.
With all the corn growing
in Sunflower County, Illinois,
you probably think it's a bit strange
we should want it in the yard too.
But the corn tassel, mister,
is my special, personal idiom.
I love to look at corn, eat corn,
and even think about corn.
What we have around here
is good corn air and good corn earth.
And you can hear corn growing:
whispering, crackling sounds.
Cornstalks, corn leaves, cornhusks,
corn silk, corn kernels —
I'll call in the wife, if you want,
but she'll side in with me.
As I said, we have four encyclopedias,
and the other books we've bought
are near to taking over the house.

TRACY LIMANTOUR:
Flowers and Smoke

A fistful of lavender lilacs
and white violets from the thick grass.
He sticks them under her nose:
"Smell them, breathe deep, Mother."
What a swell brother I have.
Mom lights up another cigarette.
"Nice, very nice, oh so nice,
now you're dirty again," she says.
Spring is blooming flowers everywhere,
but only Robby seems to care.
I love horses and yellow cats.
They never wilt in the hot sun
or shrivel up in smoky rooms.
"Don't pick any more lilacs," Mom says.
"I will if I want to," Robby says,
and bangs the door three times.

PIKE WALDROP:
For the Record

The telephone poles have flowered with posters again:
WALDROP FOR SENATOR and I LIKE PIKE.

I sit here in the White Star Pharmacy these days.
Let my old cronies yammer at the Square.

She said to me, my daughter's little daughter,
"Grandfather, they named a big clock for you."

Three thought Lincoln the best, four favored Roosevelt,
but I stuck up for Herbert Clark Hoover.

I have a gold railroad watch in my vest pocket
and a democratic hole in my right shoe.

I'm against taxes — usually; war — generally;
and sin, suffering, crime, and cor-ruption.

There are some traditional American smells here:
root beer, bacon fat, a good Tampa-made cigar.

Out at the dairy farm I have six stuffed owls
and a huge Cal Coolidge campaign poster.

The Republic is all I ever worried my head about.
Where is it now they bury the bones of circus horses?

CHICK CUNNINGHAM:
Horse Opera

Cowboy movie with John Wayne.
And I have popcorn and my gun.
But I'm still in a jail of grief.
Some ornery dude rustled my bike.

Mary Lou is a pretty keen sis.
She pats me gently on the knee.
Squaws know when a kid is down.
John's horse just got shot.

It was plenty tough out west.
You had to be right on your toes.
John sure drinks a lot of beer.
Now how can I ride to school?

My pa gets madder than John does.
He may not listen to the truth.
Indians being nasty to whites.
Take that, and that, bad guys.

GARY SHACKHAMMER:
Remembering the Thirties

The clock ticks in the hall, ticks in the hall, ticks...

Roy's Model T Ford rusts behind the mortgaged barn.
Goldenrod grows through a hole in the runningboard.

Our daddy never did come home from the turkey shoot.
"He was last seen in East Moline," says the deputy.

They say things on the farm are all going to pot.
In the towns there is a steady growth of Hoovervilles.

Huddled by the radio, we listen to Roosevelt speak.
We nod our heads and chew stale bread-heels with mayonnaise.

The morning westbound freight is crammed with men out of work.
Karl draws a NRA blue eagle on the calendar.

"Sew and sew: the whole country's gone to stitches," Ma says.
My pants are shot; Steve's coat belongs to Timothy.

Peggy's new buffalo nickel rolls down the storm drain.
Now there's nothing more that jingles in her piggybank.

Uncle Cornelius moves in with us in June.
In August we all move in with Aunt Winifred.

The clock ticks in the hall, ticks in the hall, ticks...

STELLA LYNCH:
The Opposite Sex

You bet he was there last Saturday night,
him with all that bleached blond hair,
with his thunder and lightning shirt,
with his merry-go-round pants,
with his dude-ranch cowboy boots.
He was liquored up like a payday coal miner.
He made no effort to dance with any of us.
He was looking all over for you,
asking everybody where you was at.
"Say, where's May, where's May?" he says,
popping his gum, grinning like a fool.
If you ask me, he's a real creep.
I'd like to see him mess around after me.
I got an old man and two brothers
which are all about half crazy.
They'd pour gasoline on top of him
and melt that tail of his down to the ground.
It's guys like him what take all the fun
out of these country-western dances.
There's always at least one of his type,
always someone with a Texas-size mouth
and some refried beans for brains.
If I was you, I'd stay the hell away
from the Masonic Temple, the Dew Drop Inn,
from the Sunset Bowling Lanes,
from the corner of Sixth and Main,
and the roller rink too, if I could.
But, hey, pay no mind to me, May.
There's some of you peculiar folks
who just can't wait to take on trouble.

MICHELLE TREMBLAY:
Yellow

Not cowardly,
not afraid to speak out,
and not Chinese,
no,
but yellow skin
the color of old newsprint,
or an aged sunflower
if you happen to catch him
leaning up against
a light pole or picket fence
some afternoon in late autumn.
Yellow hat, too,
and often a mustard shirt
or butter-colored pants.
We call him "Yellow,"
or "The Yellow Man."
He knows it,
he's heard it many times,
yes,
and he knows it's not because
he's scared of fights,
or bullies, or anything.
Yellow, yellow, yellow,
he's always looking like
a yellow teddy bear,
the kind you found
in your childhood attic
on those long winter Sundays.
Look, here he is now,
coming at us,
breaking in a pair
of yellow-bean shoes.

EDGAR WILSON:
Carousel

We're at the Sunflower County Fair.
I stand in noon's dusty heat.
Polly rides a spotted pony.
That's sure a catchy calliope tune.
The midway people press about me.
Sweat smells and perfume smells.
The odor of cooking grease.
There, that is *my* daughter.
I want to say it out loud.
Little kewpie doll sweetheart.
Round goes the merry-go-round.
Dizzy. I'm getting dizzy.
It must be the humidity.
Or I'm up too close.
There's laughter on the summer wind.
There's not a cloud in the sky.
Is everybody happy?
I look around and smile.
Just good Midwestern folks here.
Grant Wood's plain women.
Farmers without pitchforks.
A flock of 4-H girls.
Dentists on their day off.
Boy in bib overalls cracks peanuts.
Pink cotton candy kisses my ear.
Hot dogs and hamburgers.
Ice cream bars and ice-cold lemonade.
This is Polly's third ride.
Quite enough, I'd say.
The music stops.
The ponies stop.
But she won't get down.
Holds the reins tightly.
You got to know how to handle kids.
Use a little tenderness.

"Be Daddy's good girl."
But she screams.
"Quit that. Quit that at once."
Some nincompoop laughs his head off.
It's that bowlegged bronchobuster.
The bastard.
All right, I'll have to be firm.
I put on my mad face.
Of course the rubes are staring.
That's hicks for you.
Wonderful.
Now she's soiled her pants.
"Get down, do you hear me?"
I grab her arm and pull.
Her eyes blaze into small fires.
"I won't, I won't, I won't," she says.
Just like her mother.
Damn Dutch stubborn.
No, it can never be.
I can't love this brat.
Help!

DAVID MOSS:
  Corn and Beans

You won't believe it, Uncle Max.
The corn is already scarecrow high
and those beans are swelling up,
proud as new granddaddies.

What we have here, my boy,
is some good old-fashioned
ag-ri-cul-ture.

Corn wants to fly away, Uncle Max,
and beans want to spread their fire.

Son, the sun is surely gospel.

REV. FELIX DIETRICH:
Gospel

I'm thinking about those
boot prints up and down
the kitchen floor,
a foiled bank heist
over in DeKalb County,
and the sermon I can't write
for Thanksgiving week.
Now what is "humble"?
And what is "grateful"?
I know what chickens are:
big thundering trouble,
at least when your son
goes off and steals one.
"You don't know turkeys,"
I tell him, kind of mad.
What I told the sheriff was,
"You got lawman's tracks
from your muddy boots
right up to my freezer,
I don't hold with stealing,
and as far as I'm concerned
Bob's a good boy."
My sermon on Sunday
is going to be one I stole
off this Okie preacher
during the Dust Bowl years.
It's here in the files
along with my clippings
of the Younger brothers.

VICKI ST. CLAIR:
Home from the River

The air is green.
We walk home barefoot.
Our bodies are heavy with heat
and my nose is sunburned.
The tops of houses and trees
are scribbles on a child's scratch pad.
The river we just left
moves south in moist darkness.
A firefly lights its flare.
There is no wind.

TRAVIS JOHNSTON:
North

Haze hangs heavy in the slow September air.
A freight train crawls through parched cornfields
and past backyards strung with shirts and jeans.
A troop of sunflowers slumps across the fence.
The sour-mash sky around the collapsed silo
is the color of George Dickel's best whiskey.
Jake Cotton's barn says CHEW MAIL POUCH TOBACCO.
The bald brakeman leans from his yellow caboose
and, smiling, waves to me, and I wave to him.
Down in Tennessee I had many friendly fathers.
But I'm in Illinois now, on northern soil,
lonesome in the long shadow of Abe Lincoln's name.

RANDY WHITE:
From a Big Chief Tablet Found Under
a Bench at the Courthouse Square

Katy will only kiss me now
when we crouch among
the tall cornstalks
off Potawatomi Road.

I think she thinks she's
Pocahontas,
hiding from the gunshot eyes
that would scorch her flesh.

Last night in a hugging fog
an Illinois state trooper
roared up the blacktop
like a wild beast on fire.

Katy bit her sore lip,
and it bled
and bled
on mine.

HOWARD DRUMGOOLE:
Hotel Tall Corn

You know, I sorta, kinda like it.

It's not very tall at all,
and the only corn about the old place
is dispensed by the night desk clerk,
who's been around since Alf Landon
stopped being presidential timber.

The beds are soft, the plumbing works.

If you miss the last bus out of town,
that's where you go to get some sleep.

One cold, gloomy December evening
I slogged through half-frozen slush
to attend a wedding reception,
held in the swankiest suite they had.
The next morning the groom was found
hanging by his farmer's red neck
in a round barn west of Rochelle.

Woody Herman's band played there once,
a real "Woodchopper's Ball."

I hope it stays alive a little while.

It's the kind of rube hotel
Sherwood Anderson would hole up in
to write about the beauty of horses,
the faded dreams of small-town girls,
and the lives of lovesick millhands.

You know, I sorta, kinda like it.

GARTH LIGHT:
Muscles

I'm lifting weights in a sweaty barn.

Gail is a shy, star-kissed windmill
turning gently on a bed of air,
her long legs the color of goldenrod
under the strong and mating sun.

I'm grunting. I'm gasping. I'm groaning.

I'm Garth, her bulging lover,
a silo standing between horse and house,
steely-eyed, mute, but lovable,
a bruiser with massive thighs.

I'm building muscles I'll never use.

ARDIS NEWKIRK:
At the Charity Ball

For something to say, he said:
"I just love greenhouses and the steamy heat
and all those small plants growing tall there.
And I love woodchucks and gymnastics
and crickets and oatmeal cookies.
I can tell chicory from prairie clover.
Down by the tracks where Stacy Engle lives
there's gobs of it right this minute.
I know the names of all the townships
they have here in Sunflower County,
all the trees, and all the birds that fly around.
Do you like player pianos? I do.
The Donovans next door have one, you know.
And they start it up every now and again,
and Mrs. Donovan makes loads of lemonade,
and we shoo the flies away and laugh a lot.
They also still have their old
1928 RCA Radiola
and a chair George Ade once sat on.
I can tell swamp frogs from tree frogs.
Sure, I think Black Hawk got a bum deal.
I also think it's a terrible scandal
they have discontinued Old Settlers Day."

For something to say, I said:
"Harrison Stanley McIntyre, shut up.
You know I don't like to talk when I'm dancing!"

RICHARD GARLAND:
Railroad Strike

The radio says
the trains aren't running
for another day.

When the railroaders
go out on strike
in the dead of winter,
the frozen ground
of northern Illinois
loses its iron music.
Folks who live near the tracks
get a little jumpy.
Something familiar
has been switched off.
There is nothing now
to hold together
the body's old rhythms.

A thin, stooped woman,
wrapped in a heavy muffler
and blowing white ghosts
of zero-degree breath,
slams the back door,
flips away a cigarette,
and tips over a basket
of two dozen or so green bottles
into an empty oil drum.
The noise is like a bomb.
Across the way shades fly up.
A man slips on the ice.
Thirteen dogs bark wildly.

A blizzard wind
rattles the windows
of the abandoned caboose.

JUNIOR IVES:
Barn Burner

After Petersen's barn burned
on that warm Indian summer night,
we all sat around the kitchen table
and drank from a full-moon of apple cider,
saying "You did it, you did it,
you set fire to Seth Petersen's barn,"
pointing accusing fingers at one another
and laughing to beat the devil.
Oh, I carried on with the best of them:
with Ma and Cousin Annabelle,
with Leroy and fat Carl and Virgil,
with Uncle Roger and Aunt Alice.
And they never suspected me,
never knew why I was crazy for cold cider,
my throat parched the way it was
from the red excitement of flames,
from running across corn-stubbled fields,
my pockets bulging with matches.

LOGAN STUART:
The Union Soldier

Under a corn-green moon
on this first warm night in May,
you, our Union soldier,
throw away your rifle,
light up a brierroot pipe,
and scratch your balls.

Damnit, man, that's no way to do.
Not with the last show just let out
at the Paradise Theater,
and me all set to walk Elsie Kraft,
the new Alliance librarian,
back home down Lincoln Street.

And I suppose you know by now
that Joel Bothwell's little sister
is grabbing herself
a big whopping eyeful,
and the girls from the dime store
are giggling up a storm.

And see, too, Judge Otto Taylor,
over by the popcorn machine,
jabbing hysterically
with his hickory cane
and shouting: "whippersnapper,"
"hooligan," "degenerate."

Sure, I know, I know,
there's a Union soldier like you
standing tall on every courthouse lawn
in the good old Middle West.
And you're dead right,
we do take you boys for granted.

But next time you get the itch
to be noticed, my young friend,
why not sing "Lorena," say.
Oh hell, that's a Rebel song.
Well, maybe you can whistle a tune
softly through your teeth.

It seems to me we'd all kind of go
for a bit of that stuff
around these here parts,
this fractured-skull town
being so slugged with silence
and never much musical.

CHARLOTTE NORTHCOTT:
Insomnia

The moonlight on this spring night is simply dazzling.
One thousand brides are dancing in white wedding gowns.

Sixty-four coal cars clanked over the rail joints,
clickety-clacked right into Alliance, Illinois.

The latest wedding pictures fill the weekly *Gazette*.
I read all the names and hate all the happy faces.

Every last coal car was piled high with lumps of coal,
which sparkled there in the frosty March moonshine.

But where is *my* lover, *my* dreamer of marriage feasts?
Is he asleep, a moonbeam kissing his collarbone?

O you seekers of true beauty, where were you tonight
when a whole trainload of diamonds danced through town?

PEGGY DANIELS:
Moonlight Yodel

"In the pale moonlight" is a cliche,
so I won't use it in my down-home poem
about our stroll last night across your farm,
a stroll that took us to corncribs,
roll of barbed wire, rusted water pump,
cedar trees, stacked elm logs, orchard grass,
small hill of shelled corn, tumbleweed, mailbox.
I won't use "stroll," either, by golly,
because that's a word a bit too cute
for an outback Illinois word slinger.
And, come to think about it, my man,
walking-in-the-moonlight poems are old hat.
Instead, I'll write about how you woke up
the Beauchamp family, a dozen dogs,
sixteen cats, and who knows how many birds,
when you proved to me you could yodel.
"I'm from Yellow Medicine County," you said,
as if that explained the whole thing.

JEREMY FORQUER:
The Smell of Lilacs

I took the shortcut across the park.
The dew soaked my new suede shoes.
Through the green dusk I saw your yard light.
I could smell lilacs everywhere.
Someone was playing a piano.
That's my Stephanie Jane, I thought.
I knocked on the kitchen door.
The house was full of strangers.
They all said they didn't know you.
I walked back to the hotel.
A low branch scraped my forehead.
Sudden tears welled up in my eyes.
I should have written, should have phoned.
Three years of my life withered on the grass.
A crippled dog nipped at my heels.
I hate the smell of lilacs.

MAURY CHASE:
Famous

One time while waiting for a haircut,
I read a story in some magazine
about how this famous American painter,
Thomas Hart Benton, no less,
chewed Days Work tobacco,
and having taken up watercolors
and aiming to get at oils, too,
wondered if that would help me somewhat
in my life's one big ambition.

Well, I bought a supply of the stuff
and got right down to work,
doing a picture of a pickle crock,
slaving there under the tulip tree,
braving the insects and the summer heat,
and then it was finished
and it was very, very good,
so I kept on chewing and spitting
and won second prize at the Art Fair.

To be famous you got to know how.

SONNY BAXTER:
Spider Webs

I hunker on the porch
and stare at spider webs.
They tell me Father hated Jews
and Jews hated Father.
Now what is that to me?
I run my middle finger
over the bottom step
where the wood's gone mush.
Shoes, you clomp and clomp.
Shoes, you keep on coming,
going nowhere,
returning from nothing.
A crimson maple leaf
falls on my outstretched hand.
I tear it with my teeth,
then chomp it,
chew it to bits.
It was too beautiful.
It put a hurt high in my heart.
Grandpa crosses the grass,
the *Chicago Tribune* at his hip.
The old boy has chicken legs
and his nose is hard to blow.
The sunlight hangs dusty.
I can smell cat shit
and a cheap cigar.
There's nonsense in the kitchen.
Can't Grandma laugh her age?
Spider webs are evil.
They trap the unwary,
the too adventurous.
Spider webs are wrapped around
Alliance, around Illinois,
around the whole U.S. of A.

I stretch flat on my back
and listen to Baptist bells
and the wham-bam
of slammed doors.
Mother always went to church
in her gaudiest glad rags.
Father mowed the lawn
or stuck those watery eyes
in the bowels of his Chrysler.
No, Sunday's nothing special.
I aim to keep it so.

TOM RANDALL:
Under a Gigantic Sky

There's a milkweed butterfly
kissing Barbara Allen's knee.

Yep, I'm going to fall in love again.

We live near a burned-out roller rink,
the Chicago and North Western tracks,
and a field of tornado-toppled corn.

Barbara Allen sleeps in the shade
on the warm, pine-scented grass.

Oh, man, it hurts me so good.

We have been here forever in this place,
drifting under a gigantic sky,
lost on the golden prairies of America.

A breeze lifts Barbara Allen's skirt
above her hips, above her head.

Wow!

The whole damned Middle West
is looking
up.

VERNON YATES:
Talking About the Erstwhile Paperboy
to the Editor of the *Alliance Gazette*

Mister, he was an awkward, gangly son of a gun
and, if it's truth you're asking for,
just a little bit on the homely side too.

He whipped around here on a battered blue bicycle,
making faces, doing tricks on the handlebar.
What a cutup that kid was, a genuine show-off.

He was kind of sweet on my Penelope for awhile,
until the Turner twins, Ted and Tod, put him straight.
They told him to go peddle his papers, and we all laughed.

The boy was sure reliable, I'll say that for him.
No one on Prairie Street ever had to beg the headlines.
It's a real shame he's dead, and so young.

He was with a patrol behind the enemy lines, it seems.
They got ambushed by the gooks and chopped to pieces.
That's all I know, that's all I heard.

Well, I'll always see him there in the old news depot,
rolling up those Chicago dailies and shouting,
"You'll never see me in any Vietnam!"

URSULA ZOLLINGER:
Last House on Union Street

The mother, who has read all the Latin poets,
sitting in a wicker chair, mending old socks,
waiting for a cooling breeze, skirts hiked up.

She was paying no attention to —

The two children, who have read all the Oz books,
sitting on a bench, trying their best
to eat a whole box of chocolate-covered cherries.

They were paying no attention to —

The father, who has read all of Ring Lardner,
sitting on the porch steps, smoking thin cigars,
lighting kitchen matches with his thumbnail.

He was paying no attention to —

The college boy, who has read all of Marx,
sitting in the hammock, dreaming up a scheme
to sell *Praying Hands,* the framed *Blond Jesus.*

GLENN TWITCHELL:
Rose Petals

Look, I can't help it any if Lola Jean
chews on those pale pink rose petals
when she walks to the Catholic church
or downtown to buy a spool of thread.
And I can't worry no more that son Jack
may swallow his chaw of bubble gum
while playing tag with the Tyson kids.
Aunt Rhoda said it right, all right:
"This family of yours is never, ever
without something in their mouths,
something dangling, something dancing.
Kitchen matches, ice cream sticks,
a wad of paper, a blade of grass,
anything to bite on, anything to suck."
That's right, auntie, my mouth is dry,
my teeth itch, my lips are lonesome.
Nails, pencils, toothpicks, car keys,
they are all here when I need them.
"We got any lime lollipops left?"
says my wife, rummaging a candy sack.

PERRY MEEK:
Wife Killer

Now please pay attention, children.
The cedar chest
that Daddy has put down in the cellar
is not to be played with,
not to be used in hide-and-seek
or in any of your other games.
I hope this is clear, children,
for I don't want to have to get mad
and use my leather belt on you again.
Just pretend there's a blue monster
sleeping in that chest
who loves to eat little boys and girls.
Let's make this our new game, shall we?
And I'll play with you.
I'll be scared of the monster too.
And no more nonsense, children,
about Mother having fun with us,
keeping quiet, waiting to be found.
Damn it, I told you a thousand times
that she's not here anymore.
She's away, visiting in Vincennes.
That's where Grandma lives.
Remember?
Again, keep out of that cellar.
Do you understand me, John?
Do you, Miss Prudence?
Well, say something.
Answer me!
Oh my, oh my, oh my.
Daddy's losing patience, children.

DENISE WATKINS:
Some Come Running

When she comes in from school,
I kiss her cold, bright cheek,
she having walked the six blocks home
in February's near-zero weather,
or probably not walked at all but ran
and maybe ran almost all the way,
but did not run because it was cold and February
but ran the way a child will run
when she's happy about school or home or both
and wants to shorten the time between the two,
happy to be at either place
and wanting you to know it's true.

And so she is standing here
just a little out of breath,
warming now in the oven-warm kitchen,
and I pull off her boots for her
and help her with her coat,
and then get out the silver Christmas comb
to comb the fierce tangles from her hair.

We are deep in the middle
of a long, quiet afternoon.
There is nothing planned or scheduled,
nothing special for us to do.

But that's all right, that's good too.

AUGUST CRABTREE:
Simple Words

Plowed, seeded, cultivated, reaped:
I knew her all her life and most of mine,
her life being here on the farm, she being my wife.

She was simple, even simple minded,
so I will use simple words to simply say:
Judy was good enough to marry, good enough to bury.

EMMETT BEASLEY:
Man Talking to Himself

Brown cigars beat green cigars.

You are a fool out of Faulkner.
A farmer finding the general store closed.

Another game? Sure thing. Cut the cards.

No more baseball on the radio.
Nothing to eat but instant grits.

Too lazy to put up storm windows.

"She was an old and furious child."
I read that somewhere.

The piano smells like a coffin.

Forget the dirty dishes, the soiled shirts.
When the fog lifts, we'll go for a spin.

Gone. The wife is gone and gone for good.

Man, easy there on the beer.
Just three cans left.

Let's hear it now for bachelorhood!

RUDY GERSTENBERG:
Memo to the Erie-Lackawanna

This is awkward for me to say,
but I feel I must inform you
that your shabby boxcar 68401
passed through Alliance, Illinois,
just a little past noon today.
It looked like an Old West saloon after a brawl,
or, better, the left field fence at the ball park.
What was particularly embarrassing
was that it was coupled between
a classy Santa Fe refrigerator car
and a shiny Illinois Central coal car.

If there was ever a boxcar
with its pants down, so to speak,
your old 68401 was it, for sure.
Both doors were slung open wide
and some clown had written the usual "clean me"
and, of course, "Kilroy was here"
in the plains of interstate dust.
Now, I want you to know, too,
I'm in love with the Erie-Lackawanna.
But beat-up 68401 sure left me blue,
and I ended up feeling railroaded all day.

DR. MALCOLM LINDSAY:
Catfish and Watermelon

All day we stared at the river,
in a boat blessed with fish luck
and this woman's enormous breasts.
Now, in a tiny clapboard house
hidden by willows and trumpet vines,
mammoth Millie fries channel cat.
"How do you like it?" she asks me.
"My new scarlet nightgown, I mean."
"You're a sternwheeler caught fire,"
I tell her, "a real conflagration."
She laughs and the floorboards creak.
Wonderful! — 300 pounds of female
shaking up a sudden summer storm.
When she quits it's time to eat.
Later, after the fish are just bones,
I knife open a ripe watermelon,
broad striped and thumping good.
Millie picks out a whopping piece
and goes to work with gold teeth.
The juice runs off her double chin
and trickles between hills of flesh.
She kisses me on my sunburned neck
and then bites a black seed away
that was sticking to my right ear.
She smells of islands in the sun
and old boats soaked in morning mist.
No, it's not half bad at all
to be in love with mammoth Millie,
a river gal twice my size.

LUCY BETH YOUNGQUIST:
The Reunion

After the turkey, oyster dressing,
cranberries, creamed onions, yams,
nuts, fruit, pumpkin pie, and coffee,
Father takes off his Sunday shoes
and stretches out on the davenport,
giving us strict instructions for
no singing, no dancing, no loud laughing.
He quickly drops off to deep sleep,
the unread society page tented
over his fat and snoring face.

The stuffed common barn owl
gathers dust in the attic now.
It finally made Father nervous
after all those years of saying,
"But I love him, he's good company."
And like this puffy-cheeked bird,
the relatives that have come here today
for our big Thanksgiving reunion
are sent to the limbo of "who cares."
Father likes to eat and be alone.

WALLY DODGE:
The Hat

He sure had a mess of fishhooks on that hat.
Of course he didn't have it on his head,
because he was still working, working hard,
still on duty at Fred's gasoline station.
No, that hat of his was there on a telephone book,
right under the rack of highway maps.
Yes, I picked it up and looked at it, yes,
but not to look over the fishhooks.
It was the hat itself I was curious about,
having never seen a yellow hat with a green brim
and wanting to see what the label would tell me.
Who stole the hat is something I couldn't say.
I don't fish myself, and the hat didn't fit.
So I spent the rest of the day looking at tires
and watching a Jaguar get a grease job.
Say, is there anything special about that hat?
Maybe those fishhooks were made out of silver.
Or maybe the hat was imported from Peru.
I know it's no big joke to you, you being his wife
and having to live with an unhappy hatless man,
but I can't cry about it now, can I?

JOHNNY WILCOX:
In the Barbershop

He spits tobacco juice
on the baseball news.

I stick chewed bubble gum
in the comic books.

He wears a greasy hat
and pants with no belt.

I wear a snake-head ring
and socks that don't match.

He comes hot from corncribs
cussing out bankers.

I come damp from poolrooms
talking down hustlers.

He was a circus bum
who wrestled a bear.

I was a shoeshine boy
who married a whore.

He did two years in jail
and clobbered a cop.

I went to reform school
and flattened a priest.

They know us in this town.
We kick up the dust.

GROVER ELY:
Ancestral Home

Rebecca Ann, her head wrapped in a polka-dot scarf,
leans over the balcony and shakes out a patchwork quilt.

Down in the yard the sundial has died of too much shade.
But the white oak is a landmark, the town's pride.

All four chimneys are unsafe and haven't smoked in years.
Stepping-stones to the grape arbor are thick with moss.

I sit in the summerhouse, sip a glass of good port,
write in my journal, read the stories of Mark Twain.

Behind me, a creaky wooden gate shuts with a ghostly click.
Two or three red-orange blossoms drop off the trumpet vine.

Later on we will drink green tea and talk about the past.
On the piecrust table is a Bible with a golden key.

The ancestors who built this monumental brick home
still stare, thin lips pursed, from their oval frames.

We, the living Elys, are softer, poorer, sadder, but
we try to stay on another year, bear another Ely child.

TRUDY MONROE:
Saturday Afternoon on Elm Street

In the green-shuttered Victorian house
the birthday party boys and girls
are playing pin-the-tail-on-the-donkey.

But the real jackass on Elm Street
is the vacuum cleaner salesman next door
who has locked his keys inside the Plymouth,
the headlights burning, the radio on,
the slain deer still tied to the hood.

The salesman's face is three shades of blue.
He walks around and around the car,
turning his shapeless hat in his hands.

The donkey is full of laughing pins.

HERBERT TOMPKINS:
The Crippled Poet's Dream

I was trying hard to write this long Civil War poem,
moving closer to the Battle of Wilson's Creek.

She was tired of her lime-green lollipop,
dropping it in a scramble of honeysuckle vine.

I was busy, wrapped in thought, deep in hot Missouri,
reviling all the wrong maps and regiments.

She was finished with her picture of the old house,
saying it was very sad we had to move away.

I was confused, blinded in a smoky cornfield,
losing my weapon, tearing my Yankee shirt.

She was digging a doll's grave for Hannah Minerva,
repeating that strange and musical name.

I was sure we were all dead now, lost in time's fable,
dreaming of leafy rivers under our sycamore tree.

JOE SPRAGUE:
Fourteen Stones

Late summer hollyhocks grow on both sides
of an ornate iron fence
that separates Blackberry Hill Cemetery
from a row of rural mailboxes.

The names on the boxes
have been carefully lettered.
There must be no mistakes made here.
Everyone wants what is coming to him.

Whipping up the yellow dust
on my way home for a bean sandwich,
I stop my Dun-Rite Dry Cleaning truck
to reach for two magazines and a gas bill.

In the crowded graveyard,
where the bones of four generations lie,
there are fourteen Spragues
carved on fourteen stones.

I'm no longer worried about bad news
concealed in flowered envelopes,
for my kinfolk are all gone now
and my own fate waits across the fence.

NOAH CREEKMORE:
Bingo

Because I have little choice in the matter,
I drive my silent wife downtown.
Stores on the Square burn night lights,
but the movie marquee is brightly lit.
"Fools' Parade," I say, my voice rising,
"a real humdinger with Jimmy Stewart."
She says nothing, grips her purse tighter.
We slip past FALSTAFF, REXALL, EAT
and turn sharply into South Fifth,
stopping at an ancient red-brick building,
with its scrolled cornices, its roof of pigeons.
The American Legion Hall is where we are,
where the town plays bingo on Tuesday nights.

And the voices are calling back and forth
in the cold-snap September darkness:
"Call me when you're ready, Cary."
"Wish me luck, Wally, lots of good luck."
"Don't spend the food money, Freida."
Car doors slam, shoes scrape the sidewalk.
My wife nods grimly, says "Same time, Noah."
I drive back toward the empty Square,
in need of male laughter, a dirty joke.
The Courthouse clock is lost in fog.
I pass up EAT and REXALL again,
but pull up to the curb at FALSTAFF,
the neon a warm and friendly glow.

POP GAINES:
After the Farm Auction

I wanted to bring back some useless thing,
some utterly unusable, used-up thing.
What can you or I do with a butter churn
that will never churn butter again?
Exactly, you are absolutely correct, old woman.
Nothing, nothing at all.
Go ahead and laugh, make yourself sick.
So I don't know what I'm doing, is that it?
Did I buy the white china doorknob?
Or the emerald-green cathedral relish jar?
Or the Dolly Dingle paper dolls?
Or the mezzotint of St. Francis feeding squirrels?
For old times' sake and for mercy's sake,
no I did not, nor the Boston rocker, either.
The butter churn goes on the kitchen table.
Leave it there, leave it be.
Now then, when is the next farm auction?
I may be needing a coffee grinder next.

YALE BROCKLANDER:
Tractor on Main Street

Pay attention while I tell you this:
That beat-up, manure-stained Farmall tractor
you see parked in front of Jake's Tap
is the same Farmall tractor
that was parked in front of the bank yesterday.
Get used to seeing it all over town,
because Tom T. Cassedy won't be put off
just because some lady judge up at the Courthouse
took away his driver's license
for driving drunk into a tree.
Now, a Farmall tractor is not a Lincoln
or even an International pickup,
but as Tom T says, "it's transportation."
He's a persistent cuss, that old coot is.
His face may say "ignorant,"
but his eyes say "devious."
He knows more than one way to get in to town
for a snort or two, or three, or four.

FLOYD NYE:
Dog on the Stairs

To live in the second oldest house
in Alliance, Illinois,
is to be aware of many ghosts.
Sometimes late at night,
when a storm is blowing the trees about,
I'll sit up in the big tester bed
and hear the very first man of this place
whisper to his good wife,
who is half-asleep in a lace cap,
"Is that the dog who just went *thump* on the stairs?"
And she'll scratch her right arm and say,
"It's only the wind, Willard."
But I'll get up and go see, anyway,
even though 2:16 a.m. on March 2, 1853,
is a long, long time back,
and the last dog we had
died five years ago this month
under the wheels of a Mayflower van.

DEWEY CLAY DOYLE:
Sleeping Bags

We have a resurfaced road smelling of tar,
a black-eyed susan that escaped the grass fire,
a harp of willow leaves playing the same old tune.

Beyond a field of Shetland ponies cropping red clover,
the morning sun reddens six barn windows.

I have lived around here all my life.

By the yawning mailbox I yawn again
and try to rub the night crumbs from my eyes.
Then when my ride comes along and stops,
I gather up a heavy lunch pail,
a thermos of Susanna's strong coffee,
and *Wild Horse Mesa* by Zane Grey.

Another working day, another day to go to work.

In thirteen minutes I'll be in Alliance
to help make some more sleeping bags.

My name is Dewey Clay Doyle.
You can see it right up there
where I spelled it out with care on the water tank.

LOUISE CATHCART:
Hearing an Old Song Again

You don't have to tell me that.
That was "As Time Goes By."
And I know it was a great song
and once warmed up all
the cold kitchens and parlors
in this wind-bitten town.
I used to be happy
as day-old chickens
peeping in a splash of sun-dust
when I'd hear that love tune
on my daddy's new Philco.
But later on it made me sad
because I'd remember the boy
who used to say to me,
his arm around my neck,
"That's our song, lover girl,
and don't you forget it."
Then, just like that,
he moved away to Sioux Falls
and I never saw him again.
That was "As Time Goes By."
You don't have to tell me that.

MARCUS MILLSAP:
School Day Afternoon

I climb the steps of the yellow school bus,
move to a seat in back, and we're off,
bouncing along the bumpy blacktop.
What am I going to do when I get home?
I'm going to make myself a sugar sandwich
and go outdoors and look at the birds
and the gigantic blue silo
they put up across the road at Motts'.
This weekend we're going to the farm show.
I like roosters and pigs, but farming's no fun.
When I get old enough to do something big,
I'd like to grow orange trees in a greenhouse.
Or maybe I'll drive a school bus
and yell at the kids when I feel mad:
"Shut up back there, you hear me?"
At last, my house, and I grab my science book
and hurry down the steps into the sun.
There's Mr. Mott, staring at his tractor.
He's wearing his DeKalb cap
with the crazy winged ear of corn on it.
He wouldn't wave over here to me
if I was handing out hundred dollar bills.
I'll put brown sugar on my bread this time,
then go lie around by the water pump,
where the grass is very green and soft,
soft as the body of a red-winged blackbird.
Imagine, a blue silo to stare at,
and Mother not coming home till dark!

HAROLD BLISS:
Questions and Answers

On my way up to the post office for stamps
I stop awhile in front of the pet store.
Heinz Kleinofen is on a wobbly ladder,
washing his dirty, rain-streaked windows.
"Do you have any rabbits left?" I ask him.
"Bon Ami," he says. "You can't beat it."

Heinz is married to Bertha, a deep thinker
who thinks she looks like Ingrid Bergman.
Surrounded by eighty red teddy bears,
Bertha always lounges in bed till noon.
"How's the good wife these days?" I ask him.
"Swedish," he says. "She can't understand it."

In June, Heinz decides to get far away.
He wants to see the Grand Canyon, alone,
to forget about Bertha and the pet store.
When he returns, I inquire about the trip.
"Did you thrill to the big hole?" I ask him.
"Gila Bend," he says. "I can't believe it."

PEARL INGERSOLL:
Homework

Three telephone calls,
a chocolate doughnut,
look for lost textbook,
one hour of television,
a pickle, an apple,
Masters's "Petit, the Poet,"
two telephone calls,
a piece of pumpkin pie,
hot bath, shampoo,
Robinson's "Richard Cory,"
Frost's "Fire and Ice,"
a banana, a root beer,
Sandburg's "Chicago,"
another telephone call,
paint toenails red,
Lindsay's "The Congo,"
find lost gym shoes,
corn muffin and milk,
Pound's "Ancient Music,"
Moore's "To a Steam Roller,"
put hair in curlers,
shave legs, brush teeth,
half hour of television,
smoke a Kool cigarette,
Eliot's "Ash Wednesday,"
to bed after midnight.

NELSON HURLBUT:
   Last Day of Summer Vacation, 1924

The yellow-dog sun rolled over again
as my brother and I, cheeks rosy as peach stones,
galloped cornstalk ponies toward the shady house,
each of us with a corncob gun
going *bang, bang, bang, bang, bang.*

And perched on our mother's grapevined porch
was the third grade teacher fanning her face
with a sumac-red spelling book,
her gray hair swaying like an orchard cobweb,
and she was shouting, ''Whoa, horse, slow down there.''

Then our deep groans rose up with the dust,
we boys seeing that ancient schoolmarm
brandishing the dreaded speller weapon,
and we dropped corncob guns
and left our limp cornstalk ponies for dead.

STEPHEN FROMHOLD:
Freight Trains in Winter

In cheerless December
two trains pass each other
on the empty prairie,
their cars fired with color
from the going-down sun:
cherry red, pumpkin orange,
corn gold, lima bean green,
two strings of Christmas lights
pulled across the white rug
of a cold winter day.
And all I can say is:
Let's do it one more time.

CURLY VANCE:
The Pool Players

The tavern is down by the C&NW tracks,
across from Spencer Purdom's grain elevator.
The time is about eleven o'clock
on a snowbound Saturday night.
The pool table is made of northern red oak,
scarred by many railroaders' knives.
But the green felt is good
and the numbered balls run true.
The game is stripes and solids,
or "big balls" versus "little balls."
The menacing black eight-ball is left for last,
when the game is on the line.
The teams are made up of me
and Texaco Cap, from nearby Goodenowville,
shooting against Orange Boots
and that human scarecrow Sycamore Slim.
The stakes are bottles of beer,
the winners collecting after each game.
The other guys drink Pabst Blue Ribbon.
I insist on Grain Belt.
The break is won by our side,
but I can put nothing in any of the pockets.
The balls are spread all over the cloth.
Orange Boots is licking his chops.
The audience consists of two noisy drunks
wearing monogrammed bowling shirts
and a Mexican section-gang worker
who keeps saying, "No, no, don't shoot that one."
The smoke hanging over the table
is from my Washington, Missouri, corncob pipe
and Sycamore Slim's El Productos.
Texaco Cap chews Beech-Nut.
The luck runs all one way.
Sycamore Slim's tricky bank shots

are dropping balls into every pocket.
Texaco Cap is getting hot under the collar,
steaming like a baked potato.
The fight begins when I tell Orange Boots
to lay off banging the overhead light shield
with his goddamned cue stick.
Orange Boots says, "You gonna make me?"
I hit him hard on the side of the head
and Texaco Cap hits him with the nine-ball.
Then there's lots of shoving and wild swinging.
The bartender goes for the telephone.
The cops arrive in no time at all.
Sycamore Slim is last seen
running down the C&NW tracks
with four cold bottles of Pabst Blue Ribbon,
two bags of Beer Nuts, and a Slim Jim.

MISSY UMBARGER:
Stories in the Kitchen

The things she'd tell us were things we'd never heard of.

"Missy, you were born at home in a big brass bed.
Yes, a Hampshire boar and two two-horned Dorset lambs.
Karl, my older brother, was the troublemaker.
It was hopscotch, jacks, kick-the-can all summer long.
There is no photograph I know of of Aunt Ruth.
The garage was decorated with license plates.
I'd pick yellow flowers off the cucumber vines.
Ace Van de Vere used to drown himself in bay rum.
Daddy got sore and left Dallas out of the will.
Sister Cleo took care of a few red chickens.
We'd go by streetcar for a picnic in Barr's woods.
A chili supper in the church basement was fun.
The best friend I had was Vida Gum from Beardstown.
Vida it was who gave me this cameo brooch.
Later, Reverend Barnes quit to drive a milk truck.
We'd wade in Logan's Creek holding our long skirts up.
I recall Cleo lost Mother's new blue Bible.
Dallas moved to Canada and never came back.
Lordy, you could smell Ace coming a block away.
Our garden went uphill and ran mostly to beans.
The plates were half Wisconsin and half Illinois.
No, Ruth never let Uncle Paul snap her picture.
How I wish I could remember those jump rope rhymes.
Good heavens, Karl went to jail one time for mail fraud.
Right, boars and lambs at a Sons of Norway auction.
Missy, your hair was the color of dry corn shocks."

Grandma Ford was always fat and full of stories.

EUGENE CLARK:
Grass Roots

The old lady who told me about
the quarter moon on the outhouse door
is dead now, dying of kidney failure.
My failure is I didn't ask her
more about hokeypokey Calhoun County,
the county with no railroad tracks.
What I did ask was where she got
those blue suspenders she always wore,
the ones with the playing cards on them.
She said it was none of my business
and banged two Kennedy half dollars on the bar,
yelling for Bernie the friendly barkeep
to give her another beer and a shot.
The old lady who told me about
the quarter moon on the outhouse door
isn't going to tell me anything new,
and it will no doubt be a long wait
before someone opens up his mouth
in this down-by-the-tracks tavern
and pours out some thrilling stories
concerning the dark and damp provinces
of downstate Illinois, including
up-to-date dope on hog cholera
and yesterday's rain in Prairie du Rocher.

BOOTH SCHOFIELD:
A Dream of Old

In this old and done-for town
all the trees and streets are old,
and the stores and houses are old.
The men and women are thin, bent, and old.
They sit on dilapidated front porches
in their very oldest old clothes
and either read old almanacs and old books
or just rock in old rocking chairs,
staring into old fading-quilt sunsets
until it is time to disappear behind old doors.
I recall stopping here in the old days
at the old stone hotel on Old Mill Street
and hearing nothing but old jokes and stories
drifting like clouds of stale tobacco smoke
over the dusty ferns in the overheated lobby.
I left muttering old oaths, feeling old myself.
Now, on this old river-fog morning,
I have returned, my curiosity rising again,
my memories turning like an old Ferris wheel,
to find the old courthouse has collapsed.
With my cane I poke about in the rubble
that is spread across the Square.
An old Mathew Brady photograph of General Grant
falls through an old and burnt-out sun.

Anyway, at least the children here are not old,
even if they do have old and sad eyes,
sing old railroad songs with old faraway voices,
and play games of tag in old side yards
among old dogs and old pussy cats.
I want to befriend them, to get to know them.
I shake a boy's hand and it crumbles to dust.
A girl in old calico has flies caked to her nose.
What is this all about? What have I done?
Startled, I scream, then I begin to weep.
The children's faces spring to old smiles.

They quickly drop old balls and old dolls
and run off like chickens in a storm
to climb old locked and rusty gates.
Sure, I know what old tricks they are up to.
They are hell-bent in scampering to old attics,
hoping to find their old Halloween masks,
which are buried deep in old steamer trunks.
You see, they don't want an old coot to think
that they too can't be old and funny.
Oh why is it always, always the children,
blessed with an old, old wisdom,
who will try hardest to please
an old and foolish stranger?

AVERY LUCAS:
Apples

It's that time of year again,
so I grab my walnut cane
and take my string bag
off the hall closet hook
and walk down Grant Street
under a blowing rain
of yellow and russet leaves.
I pass a dozen boys playing
football on a muddy lawn,
pass sumac and grapevine,
pass front porch steps
orange with pumpkins,
pass smoking leaf piles,
pass Feldkamp's lumberyard
which smells of redwood planks,
pass the empty public pool,
pass the first farm west
where a monstrous corn picker
harvests a forest of corn,
and then come at last
to an abandoned orchard
of six scrawny trees.
Here, I gather the ugliest
apples you've ever seen:
puny, lopsided, bird-pecked,
yet possessing a special
flavor all their own.
And no one knows this,
no one except me, Avery Lucas,
and I'm not telling nobody
nothing about nothing.

DELBERT VARNEY:
One-Way Conversation With a Rug Beater

Bam, bam, bam went the baseball bat.

Her pa was out in back beating a rug for his wife.
He had a neck like a wrestler and hair in his ears.
I sat on the lawn and chewed a blade of grass.
"Did you know I'm in love with your daughter?" I said.

Bam, bam, bam went the baseball bat.

The dust really jumped from that sad old rug.
He had a tattooed chest and a scar on his left cheek.
I sat on the porch and smoked a Lucky Strike.
"Did you hear I'm marrying your daughter?" I said.

Bam, bam, bam went the baseball bat.

KARL THEIS:
    The Widower Turns Eighty

Old November is novembering again.

Now whose blind and broken dog
is sprawled in that heap of brown leaves?

Somewhere beyond those dead elms
a pale woman calls my name,
but she doesn't mean me, no, not me,
for my name disappeared years ago
in a rush of November wind,
about the time I had my first stroke
and the last Burma Shave sign
was ripped out like a vile weed
on the southern edge of Sunflower County.

My body is a cracked cornstalk.
My face is dusted with crop dust.

November again and again and again.

SHELLEY BROWN:
Acorns

I was over at Olin's house for a half hour or so.
He's a big-time acorn collector now,
having given up seashells and matchbook folders,
having thrown in the towel on beer cans.
Any old kind of acorn will do him.
He's not a bit persnickety, not that boy,
any more than your average ground squirrel is.
His bedroom is under siege to an acorn army.
There are acorns stockpiled in chairs,
on shelves, on his bureau, on windowsills,
plus battalions of acorns all over the rug,
not to mention in shoe boxes and coffee cans,
even a disorderly platoon of them on the bed.
I will try not to tell you that I think he's nuts,
because I'd be caught with a bad joke.
Still, one wonders what's going on in that head,
the head that put his name on the honor roll
his first three years at Alliance High School.
When I left, he put an acorn in my hand.
"Put this in a safe place," he said.
"It's going to be a long, cold winter."

CHARLEY HOOPER:
Schoolteacher

Barefoot in the sticky June twilight,
I mow a patch of stone-jumping grass.
The girl next door makes a sick, throw-up face
and stirs her drum of burning trash.
Across the street the retired switchman
hawks and spits on a ramshackle porch.
My son, a dirty diaper around his knees,
offers me one lick of his dripping ice cream cone.
I find a moldy tennis ball near the doghouse
and bounce it off old Butler's roof.
A big decision must be made soon:
grade arithmetic papers? or drink some booze?
There have been many nights like tonight,
many hours of what to do? where to go?
And wouldn't you just know this too:
the Dodge Charger has another flat tire!

MILO FERRIS:
A Damned Pretty Rain

With his stained and shapeless hat
shoved way back on his head,
Cleghorn was telling us there was doom
if it didn't rain soon — today,
tonight, this very weekend, now.
"The corn will dry up and you'll see
what you'll be paying for steak,
pot roast, chops, and hamburger."
We all nodded, said, "Sure, Cleghorn,"
and went our separate ways,
still nodding, toward drugstore,
toward tavern, toward Courthouse.
And in two days it rained hard,
and it rained hard for two days:
lightning, thunder, downpour, deluge.
Now, a couple of days later,
we see Cleghorn coming up from the bank.
"I got me some Grade A troubles,"
he says, pushing his hat back.
"Corn is all washed out on my land.
What do I need a dozen lakes for?"
"It was a damned pretty rain,"
I tell him, real nice, all smiles.
Hutchinson winks at McCarthy
and McCarthy elbows Hutchinson.
Cleghorn spits on the sidewalk
and jams the dirty hat over his eyes.
"Damned pretty rain, my ass!" he says,
and stalks off toward his truck.

LYLE MURPHY:
Pregnant

Freida wouldn't tell her father
I was the one got her pregnant.
"He'll kill you for sure," she said.
I knew his temper, his fits of violence.
"But he'll get it out of you," I said.
"He won't let you be until he does."
So I went over to her house last night
and told him I was the guy that did it.
"Damn it, we both got stupid," I said.
He just stared at me, bared his smoky teeth,
and slapped the news across his knee.
You'll never know how relieved I was.
Then her mother walked into the room,
twisting a dish towel in her hands,
and she slapped me off the davenport
and beat me with her tiny fists.
"Look, I'll marry her," I said quickly.
But she kicked me hard in the groin
and filled my ears with, "You bastard!"
"Mothers," I said, "little old mothers,"
and I limped toward the screen door.

TERRY REESE:
Boom Boom on B Street

It was the two feet of snow that did us in.
Man, what a blizzard that baby was.
Lois, eyes hard as icicles, kept saying
she was finished with me, kaput,
was going home to Mother, getting out for good.
"Bitch, bitch, bitch, bitch, bitch," I said,
as I had been saying for weeks and weeks,
knowing we were cracking up this winter,
what with all the snow, the goddamn snow,
piling up everywhere you'd care to look,
and that our marriage had dropped below zero.
"You can keep the dog," she said.
"I hate him more than I hate you."
What an urge I had to knock her on her can.
"But I'm taking the car," she said.
I said nothing, but got out the shotgun.
She followed me outside, without her coat or hat,
the icy wind whipping her hair about.
I tell you I must have been off my nut,
about good and ready for a rubber room.
I pumped four shells into that old Oldsmobile:
the windshield, both front tires,
then lifted up the snow-capped hood
and put a blast in the carburetor.
Lois screamed and hugged the dog.
"Not him, oh not him, too," she said.
I stumbled toward her, falling once, twice,
and we tumbled in the snowbank.
Then we cried and cried, all the frozen tears
dripping down like a bad leak in the roof.
"It's snowing again," she said at last.
"We're not going anyplace," I said.
I tossed the shotgun in the wrecked car
and kissed the dog on his runny nose.

ALICIA JACKSON:
Fire Dream

The fire
destroyed
everything
I owned,
everything
except
the clothes
I was wearing
and a new
poem
I had cooking
in my head,
a poem
about
a fire
destroying
everything
I owned,
everything
except
the clothes
I was wearing
and a new
poem
I had cooking
in my head.

EARL VAN HORNE:
Monopoly

When Uncle Rex puts those big red hotels
on Boardwalk and Park Place,
it's all but over, and we know it.
He will bleed us bankrupt in no time.
So what does it matter if I own
all four railroads, the electric works,
Connecticut, Kentucky, North Carolina,
four houses on Baltic Avenue,
and an orange card to get me out of jail?

Pass me the peanut brittle, Paul.
And while you're at it, old man,
the rest of the clam dip too.

Anybody here for a round of dominoes
or a fast game of hearts?
Anybody for a long walk in the snow?

Come on, Olivia, put down the Ovaltine
and move your yellow doohickey
over to Marvin Gardens.

BARNEY PRINGLE:
Heat Wave

The house smells like we had smelly socks for supper.
Under my chair is no place for your roller skates.
Are you nuts? The Illinois State Fair in this heat?
I sure wish those cicadas would shut the hell up.
Movies, movies, movies, that's all you care about.
No, I ain't worried, a tornado would improve Elm Street.
My front name? Now what kind of dumb lingo is that?
Let your mother explain "opera house." She's old enough.
Go join the 4-H Club. It sure won't bother me none.
Don't call me a grouch, young lady, and I mean it.
What? You drinking another can of Green River again?
I'll sit here and sweat in my shorts if I want to.
Trouble is, anymore, I need a trip away from here.
Monday night, and I feel already I've worked a week.

NETTIE KERSHAW:
Pickle Puss

Moody?
Him?
Cyrus?
No.
He's never
in a good mood.
Great balls of fire,
what a grouch
my brother is.
Glum isn't the word,
nor crabby, either.
A tiny smile
would crack his face,
but you'd wait
a whole heap longer
than Judgment Day
to see one.
Moody?
Moody?
Don't make me laugh.
Cy hasn't had
a good day
since he swallowed
a chew of Red Man
behind Pop's barn,
and that
was some sixty odd
years ago.
Moody?
No.
Never.
Not
Pickle Puss.

FRED DELOPLAINE:
Illinois Farmers

We are waiting to plant corn.

not yet
too wet
not yet
too wet
not yet
too wet
not yet
too wet
not yet
too wet
not yet
too wet
not yet
too wet

We are waiting to plant corn.

EDWINA MCBRIDE:
Trademarks

Dear old Daddy was always very precise:
"The shovel is out by the Cyclone chain-link fence."
"We've run out of Glad plastic garbage bags."
"Buy Tabasco pepper sauce and Kodachrome film."
"I'm going to need more of that Sheetrock gypsum wallboard."
"Get your feet off my Naugahyde vinyl-coated chair."
Daddy has been gone close to eight weeks now.
He's up there in that all-American trademark heaven,
telling the boys all about Prestone anti-freeze,
Univac computers, Neolite soles and heels,
and the pure wisdom of using Scotchgard stain repeller.
But Mom is still here, bless her vague little heart:
"Edwina, honey, put away those kitchen doodads."
"Try on that new pink whatchamacallit I bought for you."
"I can't have your thingamajigs laying around."
"Where's that doohickey I left on the hall table?"
"We must look nice for my friend Miss whozis."
Daddy, Daddy, she's driving me crazy.
I just have to straighten out this nameless wife of yours.
She doesn't know it and she'll never know it,
but she's gotten out the Q-Tips cotton swabs,
Niblets corn, and the Electrikbroom vacuum cleaner.

AARON FICKLIN:
Brother

This is Halloween night, Andy.
The ghosts and goblins are going about,
costumed kids with their tricks and treats,
with their sacks full of candy and apples.
But I'm here, drinking from a pint of Antique,
the bourbon with the train on the label,
and gazing down at your moonlit headstone:
    QUENTIN ANDREW FICKLIN
        1949 — 1974
A cold wind is pouring stiff leaves
through the tall tree of heaven.
I smell frost and pine needles and weeds.
Oh, I feel sort of stupid coming to this place,
and, yes, a little phony too.
Still, I do like these country graveyards.
They are always so full of crazy names
and sad angels with broken wings.
Listen, boy, no one blames me for shooting you.
Just an accident, they say.
It can happen, will happen, does happen.
Not that that changes things, of course.
Well, Andy, brothers we were, sure,
but never, ever, friends, I guess.
And, if anything, being drunk as a skunk,
that's what devils me good tonight.
Hey, we sold your law books last week,
and we got a pretty fair price for them,
considering they were so beat up and all.
We hope the stamps and coins will go next.
You won't care, will you, Andy?
Boy, the other news isn't much.
Poor Bernice has got pimples real bad
and stays in her room day after day,
plunking, just plunking, your steel guitar.

Dad is grouchy and is growing a beard.
Mom is silent as a slab of cheese.
But this, this is what you should know:
I aim to hunt only with loud strangers now.
Bang. Yell. Shout. Pheasants! Bang. Bang. Bang.
Brother, the Courthouse clock strikes ten.
I'm fixing to move away in your old boots.
They fit, boy. They're my new drinking boots.
The bottle's empty. All gone. Drunk up.
I'm going. I'm walking. I'm running.
Lord, Lord, the restless, relentless moon
stalks me through a death of black corn.

JEROME HOLTSAPPLE:
Flower Thief

Mrs. Stockton must have seen me from where
she sat swinging on the front porch swing.
"What you doing picking my flowers?" she said.
"I just took one red marigold," I said.
"Well what you want it for?" she said.
"It's — it's for my girl friend," I said.
That was a lie, for I picked it for me.
"You're a little too old for that stuff," she said.
I wanted to say something real smart
or roll my eyes like Groucho Marx,
but I couldn't do it, couldn't pull it off.
"I might ring up the sheriff," she said.
"You do that now," I said, getting mad.
"A real wise guy, ain't you?" she said.
"Here's something else to get sore about," I said,
and pulled the petals off three white roses.

RACHEL OSGOOD:
Cornhusk Dolls

A warm dream of little girls
playing with cornhusk dolls
on the porch of a country house,
the sun falling in dusty slants
through a tangle of sweet-pea vines,
female chitchat and laughter,
washed and ironed cotton dresses
hugging the rough doll bodies.

Then the dream breaking up
when I awake to midwinter sleet
drumming against the windowpanes,
and again I must live without
a daughter, a worried child
who whispers sweetly in my ear,
"Have you seen my pretty dolly?
I think I left her in the corn."

CLYDE ROCKWELL:
Bus Stop

Before the thundershower,
I stared for a long, long time
at a pig-plump waitress,
waiting for her evening bus.

Corn tasseled in my groin.
My hands ripened to melons.

I'll farm where I damn please.

KEVIN PRUITT:
Taking Down the Flag

We're fifth graders now,
so all of us kids are grown old enough
to take down the flag after school.
The first afternoon, I told Freddie:
"Don't let it touch the ground.
Don't let it touch the ground.
Don't let it touch the ground."
But he let it touch the ground.
Freddie let the flag touch the ground.
I told him over and over:
"Don't let it touch the ground."
But it weren't no use,
so I kicked him hard in the butt
and called him a bad word.
I don't know why they got mad on me.
It weren't me let the flag touch the ground.

APRIL MCINTYRE:
Fishing in the Rain

I left him there,
deep in his fishing,
six little trout,
their necks broken,
stuffed in the pockets
of his denim jacket,
the last worm waiting
in a coffee can,
cold rain pelting
the sycamore leaves.

I told him goodbye.
I had had quite enough
fishing in the rain.
He caught six trout
in the leafy cold.
I caught nothing.
Deep in his fishing,
he had one worm left.
It was his worm.
I left him there.

NED SWIFT:
Downtown

Anything going on downtown, you ask?
You better believe it, my good friend.
The mail truck got in early
but went out late,
there's another huge pothole
right in front of the Mobil station,
the Grain Belt beer sign at Jake's
was wrecked sometime last night,
and a Funk's G-Hybrid seed salesman
and a retired pharmacist
from Prophetstown, Illinois,
were hammering out a new foreign policy
on the stone bench at the Courthouse.
But that's not all,
that's not the half of it.
Up at the Dairy Queen,
Jennifer Hornbeck told me
that she wouldn't speak to me again
unless I got rid of my shoes,
my jeans, and my T-shirt that says
IT TAKES LEATHER BALLS TO PLAY RUGBY.
Now, my question is:
Does she want me naked tonight
after the band concert in the Square?

ANTHONY FASANO:
Greenhorn

It was the pinball that did it,
how I went from nobody to somebody
at Harry Peacock's hardware store.
I started off pretty bad there.
I didn't fall for the left-handed monkey wrench,
but they got me with the striped paint.
Naturally I became "the greenhorn"
and had to listen to comic remarks like
"You still living in that three-story house
over that vacant lot on Union Street?"
When the lunch hour rolled around
I could hardly wait to get out of there,
to get away from the make-fun-of-the-dago jokes.
I'd go across the Square and play pinball:
ga-ga-ga-ga, goin-goin-goin-goin,
ga-ga-ga-ga, goin-goin-goin-goin.
It got to be a real obsession with me,
this playing pinball all the time.
After supper, with no one to see or be with,
I'd go into one tavern after another
and play game after game after game.
I could do everything but make those machines puke,
and my scores got higher and higher.
Then the bums at the store heard about it
and said they could take my ass
anytime, anyplace, and no fooling.
Well, they came around and they tried,
but I beat every one of them, and no fooling.
I beat Dennis, Glenn, and Irving
on every pinball machine in Sunflower County.
I killed them on the Indy 500,
murdered them on All-Star Baseball,
flattened them on the Olympiad,
and destroyed them on the All-American.

"Hey," Irving said, "is this really Tony Fasano,
our own little hardware store greenhorn?"
I shoved another coin in the Indy 500,
pulled back the plunger, and let the ball fly.
I didn't want to talk to them anymore.
All I wanted were the musical sounds of
ga-ga-ga-ga, goin-goin-goin-goin,
ga-ga-ga-ga, goin-goin-goin-goin,
and maybe all night, and maybe forever.

CRYSTAL GAVIS:
   Depressed After Being Fired from Another Job

The black ant drags a bread crumb
clear across the kitchen floor.

That's something else I can't do.

BECKY FARMER:
Seen and Not Heard

My brother he's four years old today
and I'm going on eight and a half.
We're not supposed to talk to any strangers,
but did you drop this here tomato?
We saw it laying on your grass
and wondered if you coulda dropped it.
Or maybe you threw it out,
seeing it was kinda small and yellow,
and you couldn't, wouldn't eat it that way.
I know that my brother here,
who like I say is four years old today,
won't eat nothing that's yellow,
although he ate a sorta yellow tomato
that we had for supper tonight.
But he never said a word against it,
'cause Mom and Dad they got this rule
that kids should be seen and not heard,
and if you have that same rule,
you are maybe getting mad with us
for talking to you in your yard.
So I think I'd better grab my brother
and roll him home in his wagon real quick
and let you decide about the tomato:
if it's yours or not yours
and if you think it's too yellow to eat yet.

HERSCHEL NIEDERCORN:
Requiem

Aunt Pauline was a bright lights girl,
the kind who likes hotel lobbies, noisy bars,
opera night, New Year's Eve on State Street,
and a steak approximately the size of a doormat.
When she knew she had only a short time to live,
we brought her out to the country:
muddy roads, bare locust trees, frozen lawns,
a barn full of Holstein cows, lots of kids.
She stayed in the house all winter,
telling us stories about her many travels,
playing hearts and dominoes, reading Sherlock Holmes.
By spring, she had lost a lot of weight,
and I knew the worst was soon to come.
We took one last ride in the Dodge pickup,
waved to the rowdy Callison girls
singing ''Rock of Ages'' on their screened porch,
stopped by the creek, watched the squirrels play.
Tonight she kissed Benjy, our youngest boy,
who said, ''I can belch anytime I want to.''
She died upstairs in the sewing room.
She said, ''I touched the sun on a red flower
and it was cold, so terribly cold.''
Aunt Pauline was a bright lights girl.

TERESA BIRDSELL:
Sunflower Queen

It was not the blue ribbon I wanted,
not a token to hang in the kitchen,
but just the knowing I was best,
to be tops at something for once,
some success to remember a day by,
to have a day worth remembering.
So when I won first prize
for the biggest sunflower
at the Sunflower County Fair,
I knew I had all I really wanted,
that I needed no loud praise,
no handshakes, no bear hugs,
no snapshots to paste in a book,
nor even a freckled nephew's
''Grandma's the new sunflower queen.''

I picked up my handsome champion
and kissed it the way a mother
would kiss an exceptional child,
and I patted its stiff dry head,
recalling a lost cornhusk doll.
Then I walked out into the sun,
past food tent and Ferris wheel,
and right out of the fairgrounds,
moving through rings of gnats,
crying with strange jubilation,
at peace with the cockeyed world,
at ease with myself at last.
When I came to the crossroads,
I stopped, dried my eyes,
and went back to get my sunflower.

DUSTY PICKENS:
Logan's Creek

This is what I found in Logan's Creek,
just downstream from where it serpentines
near a wildflower-covered hillside:
several bent tin cans, various car parts,
a yellow condom, a ketchup bottle,
a straw hat, an overhead-fan blade,
a pair of size thirty-two Jockey shorts,
a patchwork quilt, a spoon, a rubber boot,
and a rusty roll of barbed wire.
Barbed wire? Now what was that doing there?
Maybe some frantic farmer wanted
to fence in his own private hill,
had a heart attack or change of heart
and then left it there, for pity's sake.
Who knows. Who can tell now. Who cares.
All I know is, I don't use condoms anymore
and the name stitched in the shorts
was Maurice M. Motherwell's, not mine.

JEFFREY KOHRS:
Summer Employment

I don't want to clean out stables.
I don't want to detassel corn.
I don't want to bag groceries.
I don't want to wash dishes.
I don't want to mow cemetery grass.
I want to do what Dad did
when he was sixteen years old.
I want to spend my summer
under a '47 Chevy.
Did you hear me correct?
That's what I want to do.
I want to spend my summer
under a '47 Chevy.
"Oh, dry up," my sister says.
"You're going to work like the rest of us."
Mom says nothing, just bites her lip.
Dad isn't around, of course.
You know where old Dad is, right?
Sure you do. You bet you do.
Okay, all together now:
"He's out there in the side yard
under a '47 Chevy."

BOOG MONCRIEF:
Falling Apart

The eleven o'clock freight horns through town
and creeps across the rusted iron bridge.

Dad's abandoned mill shudders in its bones.
Windows shake at Guthrie's Feed and Grain.

I wait patiently behind crossing gates,
my head full of bedpans and blood tests.

That birch tree there at the side of Rush Road
will never make another green leaf.

No more wet dreams, few erections, no pep,
no lust for that cute county health nurse.

This ruined sidewalk crumbles to sidewalk dust.
A blind man pokes his cane in the weeds.

Hey, you want to know something funny, Faye?
I think I'm a bit too old for you.

PAUL SUMMERHAY:
Manuscript

For the best reason I know, namely,
that I don't want to talk about it,
discuss it, go over it, argue about it.
It's no more than that, that's all.
Some things are better left unsaid.
And I know you don't want to hear the news,
because it's not good news for you,
and it certainly hasn't been good for me.
Okay, I'll quit stalling around now.
It wasn't Quinlan's manuscript I left there,
in the big, bad cathouse in Chicago,
it was *your* manuscript I left there,
the collection of stories and poems.
And I can't go back there to retrieve it
because I forget where that place was, is.
All those Chicago streets look alike,
especially in the dark, when you're drunk.
So what can I do? Where can I turn?
I know what *you* can do, must do:
blow up, call me names, even punch me out.
Lord knows, Al, I deserve it, in spades.
I read through half of your manuscript,
up to where the eccentric beekeeper
throws a hive of bees into the squad car.
You write well, or at least not bad,
but I do wish you had made yourself a carbon
or saved some drafts, or something.
Look, cheer up, look on the bright side.
Maybe one of those good cathouse ladies,
out of the goodness of her cathouse heart,
will show it to some big-time publisher,
some bird just in from the East Coast,
in need of some Windy City tail.

GRETCHEN NAYLOR:
　Nowhere

"We are living in the middle of nowhere," I said.
"Well, at least we're in the center of things," he said.
"Must you always look on the bright side?" I said.

JUDGE EMIL ZANGWILL:
Angry Words

It's Friday night again in Alliance, Illinois.
I leave the Courthouse by the jail-side door.
I'm drained from endless bickerings of the courtroom,
the lies, the tears, the bloodlust accusations;
sick of sharp-tongued lawyers and dull-eyed juries.
On my way home, walking toward Liberty Street,
I stop at Bert and Larry's liquor store
to pick up a quart of Jack Daniel's black label,
then continue to plod along for another two blocks,
the April mist thickening to April rain.

Dixie, my third wife, has sued me for divorce.
Daughter Marilee has dropped out of sight,
somewhere between the Robert Street bridge in St. Paul
and the Boatmen's National Bank of St. Louis.
Son Scott writes from Stateville that prison guards
have taken his poems, his notebook of new songs.

Yes, this empty house has heard angry words too:
"cheat," "bitch," "I'll break your goddamn neck."

Gents, listen to me now and listen to me well.
Some men should always get drunk alone.

CARL YELENICH:
One Tough Hombre

I was red-faced, tight-lipped angry
for four, maybe five, whole days.
The truth is, I could have killed someone.
Later, when I started to feel good again,
I knew I was a real son of a bitch.
So I broke a bottle with my fist.
Cuts, lots of blood, some stiffness, some pain.
But it felt so good, so goddamn good.
I only get hurt when I hate myself.
And I'm one tough hombre, my boy.

BEN HILDEBRAND:
Father and Son

I can find her gravestone, son,
because I know which one is hers.
I could not forget that.

But there's no one's name on it.
I don't see Great-Grandmother's name.
Who took away her name, Pa?

Her name's Elizabeth Moss.
Time can be very harsh, my boy.
And the wind never quits.

I'll remember where it's at.
Between the big elm over there
and this gray slab that says Cobb.

Yes, Cobb here and Payne close by.
Hurlbut and Goodenow up the hill.
Proud names, old and proud names.

Did she live her whole life here,
here in Sunflower County, Pa?
Did she see Buffalo Bill?

She was born somewhere in Maine.
The ocean was what she bragged on.
But cornfields got her now.

MASON SINCENDIVER:
Driving to Town

Mr. Post,
I feel I've been poorly used,
a courtroom Bible
that's to be replaced
but which has never been read.
In my heyday
I was a walking newspaper
and an expert on quitclaims.
An almanac brain
is what I had.
Judge Lord could tell you that.
Say, you're awfully quiet, Mr. Post.
And gloomy too.
But then today
isn't much of a day, is it?
Not with the temperature still
down around zero
and this country road
slick as glass with black ice.
Now, about that position
in the county clerk's office.
Maybe you could,
perhaps, if possible,
put in a word or two
to the right people.
You know those fellows
at the Courthouse,
and they know you.
Sir, you've not heard
a word I've said.
You're not asleep, Mr. Post?
Mr. Post?

WOODY O'NEILL:
Outside the Western Auto Store

Calvin wanted to tell his story again
on how he saw the trotter Speedy Crown
capture the coveted Hambletonian,
Du Quoin, Illinois, 1971.

Look at that blonde with the big ba-zooms.

Gilbert wanted to educate us,
to let us in on everything he knew
concerning the red-legged grasshopper,
Alfalfa County, Oklahoma, 1954.

Feel 'em, fuck 'em, forget 'em, is what I say.

Bradley wanted to brag and brag and brag
about the bottle cap collection he owned
when he was just a knee-pants kid,
Baltimore, Maryland, 1938.

Now you take your average Arab girl.

Ivan wanted to reminisce a bit,
to explain the important job he once held
at the Ford Hopkins drugstore,
Cedar Rapids, Iowa, 1962.

Anybody know a nice Christian whorehouse?

SANDRA JOYNER:
Newcomer

This is the first afternoon
since moving to this flat town
I don't sweat with suspicion.

There is no one to talk to,
but the garbage man just asked
could he bum a cigarette.

I am trying now to learn
how to live with tight-lipped folks
who refuse to neighbor me.

DEREK VREELAND:
The Apple Trees of Pioneer Grove

My ring was on her finger
when I took her that day
to the village of Pioneer Grove.
We had a picnic there:
salami, a loaf of bread,
a bottle of French wine.
We walked hand-in-hand
under the yellow-apple trees,
the fruit round as full moons,
and talked about the poems
of Apollinaire and Villon,
and how to eat a lobster,
and how to sail a sailboat.
"We shall have no secrets
from each other," I told her,
and explained about Esther,
and about Rachel and the children.
"No secrets," she said,
"so I guess you should know
I've been married twice
but divorced just once."
"Damn Pioneer Grove," I said.
"Damn Apollinaire," she said,
and worked my diamond ring
off her ring-worn finger.

KIM AUSTIN:
Art Class

Be-
cause
there
was
too
much
blue
sky
in
my
real
life
pic-
ture
of
Sun-
flow-
er
Coun-
ty
I
paint-
ed
the
tall-
est
corn-
stalk
there
ev-
er
was
an-
y-
where
an-
y-
place.

LARRY GRAHAM:
Empty Beer Can

You write from Pittsfield
that you don't love me anymore.
Once when we were driving around
under a big Pike County moon
you threw a beer can
out the window of my pickup.
Tonight, 200 miles away,
it comes bouncing, end over end,
up to my front door.

RALPH C. KRAMER:
Gossip

This is what I heard them say:

"Did you ever get to know Christian Zak?
He liked to settle an argument with a brick.
Almost killed his cousin Elwood
at an Optimist picnic over to Clover Hill."

"Right, Merle Tyner's boy, that's him.
That's the one the youngest Eggleston girl
is going to marry up with next month.
Not a bright kid, but not dumb, neither.
Was in the Navy for four years, I think,
then went deckhand for some towboat outfit
pushing loads of coal up the Illinois River."

"Lamar Robinson got home late last night,
after a billiard tournament downstate,
and found the turtle had died.
He can't do it, he can't keep nothing alive."

"So he sits back in his wicker chair,
stares for a minute at the orange sun ball
sinking below the ragged cornstalks,
puffs on his Corona Western, and tells me that
twenty-three cents is still the record
for the lowest light bill in this town.
Set by the Chandler sisters in 1919, he says."

"No, I wasn't at Frank's funeral, Clara.
Jane and Cletus didn't go, either,
and they knew him better than I did.
Gracious, even the dead keep a body hopping."

"You all heard me speak of Chester Thigpen.
He fell off his tractor Tuesday week.
When I told Mother about it this a.m.,
I thought she'd never stop laughing.
They found whiskey on him, of course.
You'd think a man in his upper fifties
would learn to control hisself a wee bit."

"About you returning to Sunflower County:
another face and another name,
but mostly just another face with no name.
Am I right about that, Uncle Leo?"

Yes, that is how they said it.

SCOTT LANSING:
Trotters

High in the stands
at our county fair,
I sit beside
an old hunchback
who talks about
Sherwood Anderson,
chomp on a hot dog,
and watch trotters race.
The sulkies rush
down the final
frenzied straightaway.
Cheers curl my ears.
I spill mustard
on my scarlet shirt,
which now looks like
the sunset silks
of the glum driver
who came in last.

CAMILLE WEBSTER:
Bull Durham

You don't hardly never
see that done no more.
The man over there
under the awning
in the ten-gallon hat
and yeller silk shirt
rollin' a cigarette,
not spillin' the tobacco
from a Bull Durham sack,
and lightin' it proud like,
knowin' there's nobody
'round these parts
who can carry that one off,
and watchin' to see
who, if anybody,
has noticed what
an old smoothy cowpoke
just got off the bus
to dazzle all us yokels.
Don't he do that fine?
He sure do.

BOYD DRAKE:
Staying Up Late

A fly buzzes around the bare light bulb.
No land to farm, no fun, no road to fame.

Where is that blind girl I knew in Athens?

Blue flowers decay in this den of books.
Dead vines spell my name on the schoolyard fence.

Should I boil an egg or peel an apple?

But one thing is sure: boredom's got me bad.
My pipe weighs a ton in my smoked-out face.

Why must I feel so damned depressed again?

ADAM POSEY:
  Sunday Comics

Look, I don't want to hear about
new storefronts on Main Street,
cracked plaster in the downstairs bathroom,
the Sunflower County Cooperative,
my twenty-fifth class reunion,
what happened to last fall's Indian corn,
Ben's Union Pacific belt buckle,
who just bought a Tiffany lampshade,
when the mortgage payment is due,
Faulkner, Hemingway, and John Dos Passos,
ten cents off on lemon furniture polish,
why we need to buy a Rototiller,
who wrote "Red Sails in the Sunset,"
warped bricks at the railroad depot,
the latest Community Chest drive,
tomatoes turning orange on the vine,
ecru lace curtains and chenille bedspreads,
any hymn called "Jesus Paid It All,"
David's Black and Decker workbench,
a polyester doubleknit pantsuit,
why Mr. McCloud won't eat Quaker Oats,
toothpick holders and antique snuff jars,
what high school girl swims nude in the river,
cattails out by Butterfield's pond,
who's got an old limestone fencepost,
Comet, Ajax, or Spic and Span,
the levee at New Orleans, Louisiana,
disgruntled farmers griping about taxes,
Pittsburgh plate glass windows,
three missing packages of Kool-Aid,
the Caterpillar plant in Peoria,
what's the matter with the Chicago Bears,
Fred's poker game at the fire station,
or Why Doris Peckinpaugh left town.
I want to hear only one thing:
the Sunday paper smacking the front porch.
I can't wait to learn what's up
with Dick Tracy, Blondie, and Moon Mullins.

ELLEN OPDYCKE:
The Fall

The one-legged house painter,
my dearly beloved husband,
stands on the topmost rung
of a tall ladder that leans
against the whitest house
in Alliance, Illinois.
His cap, torn at the crown,
is spattered with brown paint
from the big job he performed
on Al Ackerman's horse barn.
But his coveralls are clean,
and a new red bandanna
hangs like a bright flag
out of the right rear pocket
where he squirrels his change.

The one-legged house painter
has been on that ladder
painting the same colonial house
for more than seventeen years now.
Through my kitchen window
I see him there every day.
Never mind the banker's wife
who fainted when he fell
and the screaming ambulance
that took him away to die.
Forget that the old mansion
was torn down last week.
And ignore, if you please,
that his favorite brush
is as hard as Rover's bone.

FAYE HOCKING:
At the Home for Unwed Mothers

Well, for one thing,
I wasn't wearing my stockings that night,
and that's where it got off wrong,
because when he touched me on the knee
I got goose bumps just like that,
and suddenly he was hardly breathing,
and a funny look came into his eyes,
like he had gotten religion real fast
under the spell of a hellfire preacher,
and he pushed me down flat to the car seat
and lifted my skirt and went on from there,
pulling and tugging at my clothes,
and I could say nothing to stop him,
and I wanted him to stop,
and I didn't want him to stop,
and it was like being on a roller coaster,
with my head getting lighter and lighter
and no way to turn back,
and then it was finished,
and he was finished,
and a kind of peace swept through me
and I accepted what had happened,
like when you have a tooth pulled
and you know there's no putting back
what's gone for good,
but I didn't love him more for it,
and I didn't start to hate him, either,
and it's only the calm cuddle of my child
that I'm wanting now,
knowing, and knowing it for sure,
that I'll never get to finish high school,
which was something I wanted too.

DAISY COLE:
   The Housekeeper's Story

The Berry sisters
must always say
the Lord's Prayer
before they go to sleep.
That's one of many firm rules
in the Berry house.
Now Jane Berry kneels,
bows her head,
and says the words
in a clear, sweet voice.
But Janet Berry never kneels,
never does it right at all.
She just jumps into bed,
pulls the covers over her face,
and mumbles like an imp.

"It doesn't make
a damn bit of difference,"
shouts Mr. Berry.
"It does so,"
screams Mrs. Berry.
And they move to the kitchen
to argue about this,
their angry voices rising
above the coffee cups.
Meanwhile, upstairs,
the girls get out flashlights
and cut the heads
off all the photographs
of Mr. and Mrs. Berry
on their wedding day.

OTIS K. SIZEMORE:
Child in the House

When my small son,
in red heat,
threw his baseball
through the hall window,
I didn't get sore,
for I was already
just as mad as he was
and about ready
to bust up the room,
what with my team,
the Cardinals,
losing 8 to 0
to the Phillies
on national TV.
So I grabbed my
Enos Slaughter
Louisville Slugger
and knocked out
two more panes of glass.
"There," I said,
"that's one for me
and one more
for you, my boy!"

WARREN EGGLESTON:
Nostalgia

I live only in the past, boy.
The present is a flat beer
I poured down the kitchen sink,
and the future is a loaded shotgun,
locked in the toolshed
with the busted power mower.
Hooray for Lincoln Zephyrs
and interurban trolley cars.
Three cheers for Jack Armstrong.
The trumpet of Harry James
is sweeter to me now
than it was in high school.
I still carry a smiling picture
of Jeanne Crain in my billfold,
and I never miss a single movie
Errol Flynn ever made.
I dream of grammer school fun,
cherry Cokes, Dick Tracy Big Little Books,
and my collection of milk bottle caps.
Bee shit on all that's buzzing around
in this falling down world.
Don't come to me with your news events,
your insane babblings
about men blasting off to the moon
or teenage singers who can't sing.
I just wish I could write
President Roosevelt
and tell him he's doing just fine
and the war is going our way,
and that I got another date
with Marjorie Jo Kincaid
to dance to Tommy Dorsey tonight.
Go get 'em, Cardinals,
beat those damn Yankees.

Touchdown for Frankie Sinkwich!
Oh, there's no doubt about it.
I'm going to stay put
in the fabulous 1940s.
Close the door, children.
Daddy doesn't know you anymore.

KEITH APPLEBEE:
Boozing Bigots

Just as the evening whistle blows at the tool plant,
 the great western sky blazes up and bleeds to glory.

But men tied to lunch pails are in a mad rush to get drunk.

Did you hear the one about the queer Injun chief and...

Forgotten wives slouch in doorways and practice their frowns.
The corned-beef hash burns, the radio blabs on and on.

Well, there was this nigger who hated watermelon and...

Any brand of beer will do, any wine, any old hooch.

Yes, sure, I used to be one of these boozing bigots.
Christ, getting smashed was the real business of the day.

JOLENE DOERR:
Fat

Not being too smart in school
is not so bad to worry me much.
Being fat is something, though.
The other kids tease me all the time:
before English, after Math,
during Gym, during lunch hour,
and any time they can get a chance.
I'm so awful sick of that dumb rhyme,
Fatty, Fatty, four by four,
can't get through the kitchen door.
I don't care what Mom and Dad will say.
I'm not going to any more schools
or sit in another class.
And I've locked my bedroom door
so they will know I mean what I mean.
The pain of fat will not quit.
It's like my life has just stopped.
I don't wish that I was dead.
But I do wish I was never born.

IVAN LOOMIS:
The Vision

I took *Tess of the D'Urbervilles* with me
to my secret place at the riverbank,
a quiet, willow-shaded spot
where the Ausagaunaskee narrows
and bends away to the southwest.
I swam in the muddy summer water,
then stretched out on the warm grass.
Soon I was asleep, with Tess in my arms.
The sun was sinking fast when I awoke,
and I saw a naked girl
come out of the shimmering river.
She looked fantastic:
dark-brown hair, big-nippled breasts,
small waist, great-muscled thighs,
deep-fleshed buttocks, plump calves,
and a face I would love till death.
Then she moved closer,
there in the sun-dazzled afternoon,
moved slowly, so very slowly,
swinging her wide hips,
her tongue licking her upper lip.
The willow leaves stopped their shaking.
There were no more insect noises
in the mouths of flowering weeds,
no nervous bird chirpings.
Everything was still as God.
I could hardly breathe.
"Tess," I said out loud, at last,
"I'll have to take you home now.
You've got me much too excited,
and Mr. Hardy doesn't know where we are."

ELWOOD COLLINS:
Summer of 1932

On sticky summer Sunday afternoons
there would be lots of people
standing around in the yard,
mostly relatives and neighbors
in cotton dresses and white shirts.
They would come and go until dusk,
talking, talking, talking, talking
about jobs, bread lines, foreclosures,
about Hoover and Roosevelt,
about the latest layoff or suicide.
Someone, usually my father
or one of my unemployed uncles,
would be scratching in the dirt
with half a hoe or ragged rake,
not to plant, not to cultivate,
but to be doing something, to be busy,
as if idleness was some kind of dark shame
or red pimple of embarrassment.
I was there, too, a silent child
with my blue wagon and blue spade,
making little mountains of dirt
and patting them down with my fist.
When the lemonade ran out,
my mother or a maiden aunt
would bring out a pitcher of water
and someone would always say,
"You can't beat good old water
when you have a terrible thirst."
The Ford in the driveway was ours.
It was leaking oil, drop by drop,
and the battery was dead.
We were obviously going nowhere.

LANCE BOOMSMA:
Wedding Reception

"Hey, go kiss the bride," I said to my brother Ben.
"I already done that already," Ben said.
"Where is it you're to honeymoon at?" Mother said.
"Galena," my bride said. "Up to Galena."
"You ain't sore she was once your girl?" I said to Ben.
"That's the way life goes," Uncle Ted said.
"Galena?" my sister said. "Why Galena?"
"Cold there this time of year," Aunt Flo said.
"We'll be back in a week," my bride said.
"Better take plenty of sweaters," Mother said.
"'We're going via Rockford and Freeport," I said.
"How about that? First class all the way," Ben said.

PHYLLIS NESBIT:
Chinese Restaurant

At our town's Chinese restaurant,
one Chinese blue neon letter
has just given up the ghost.
MOO CHOW'S now reads MOO COW'S.
Does Moo care? Is he perturbed?
"No," he says, "Moo care only
if folks don't eat chow at Moo Chow's."
"You mean Moo Cow's," I said.
"Chow, cow, plow, sow," he says.
"Moo Chow don't give Shanghai shit."

O. E. MOONEY:
Working on the Railroad

Well, here I am in a Rock Island caboose,
eating bread and onions for lunch
and watching a heavy midsummer rain
steam on the Middle Western streets.

"Be good," said Mark Twain,
"and you will be lonesome."

Cold rain in Culpeper County, Virginia.
I was alone and silent there also.

I know how the talk goes, what they say:
"That Mooney, he's no damn fun, you know.
He won't gamble, won't take a drink.
Standoffish, that's what he is."

Why can't I swear, knock a man down?
The railroad is the only body I've bruised.

I need a bad woman to be bad with.
But I'm Mooney, the shy onion eater.

HOPE GIBBS:
Fire and Water

We were down again
on a fishing Sunday
to Kankakee, Illinois,
bitching as usual
about the river
you called filthy.
It has already been
a dozen or more Septembers
since you were there
in that old town,
flat on your back
at Borg's rest home,
Uncle Herbert's picture
on the bedside table.
I heard from the Swede
you were hemorrhaging
when that awful fire
broke out in the kitchen.
They carried you, he said,
from the second floor
and put you under
the white oak tree.
You died there,
smelling the smoke
of burning drapes
and cheap paint,
your last thoughts
turning perhaps
to the clear, cold waters
of a long ago
Canadian childhood.

ROBERT EVERWINE:
Son

Hell no, she's not pregnant,
she's just plain fat.
And here she comes now,
back from a trip to the store,
hair in her eyes,
a swelling mosquito bite
decorating her forehead.
''Norma,'' I say to her,
''you're really a sight.''
Her chin quivers
and she bites her lower lip.
The bag of groceries
crashes to the kitchen floor.
A can of sockeye salmon
rolls under the table
and smacks against the stove.
She begins to cry.
I kiss her once on the nose
and twice on the mouth,
then we climb the steep stairs
and make love on the bed.
We keep on trying.
Year after year
we keep on trying and trying.
But poor, patient Norma
never gets pregnant.
Look, she just wants a baby.
I want a son!

NATHAN ACKERMAN:
In Kreb's Kandy Kitchen

Now don't forget, Lefty, to look me up
when you want those wisdom teeth yanked.
I'm above Western Union, in the McFee Block,
and in Yellow Pages my name is number one.
There's no need to hurry, just take your time.

You say you've been in pain now and then?
But it's not a tooth, nothing up there in the head?
What? Your pitching arm is where you hurt?
Coach Claypool blames it on your bum teeth?
You yelp like a crazy when you throw the ball?

Maybe it's your teeth, and maybe not, my boy.
I'll check it out, but for right now,
come over to the window and open your mouth.
No, Lefty, first take the jawbreaker out,
and the jelly bean too, while you're at it.

DOROTHY TILLINGHAST:
Local History

They asked me to dig up the dope
on our local Indian tribe.
I found nothing, nothing at all,
not even a paragraph in
Story of Sunflower County.
So they brought in a professor
from some fancy eastern college.
The big man arrived on the scene
with an electric typewriter
and a ream of yellow paper.
In three days he had the job done.
Last Sunday there were two columns
of his scholarly conclusions
stuck in the *Alliance Gazette,*
under the predictable head:
WHITE SETTLERS CHASE OFF INDIANS.
Lies, lies, lies, lies, nothing but lies.
But, at least, we are up to date,
a proper American town,
and our newly discovered ''guilt''
will never trouble our future.

TINA ROMERO:
The Jesus Barn

The *Jesus Saves*
on Kentfield's
fine red barn
fights despair,
evil thoughts,
carnal lust,
but who will
save the barn
from hell's fire
on this night
of whiskey,
loose women,
raucous song?

Yes, Jesus saves,
but not on
this sad time
when mad drunks
whistle through
summer weeds
to torch up
the Jesus
barn of steers,
their hot heads
full of hooch,
their lost souls
black as sin.

CORKY NOLAN:
High School Blues

Basketball game. We win. The Cornhuskers win.
Now the parking lot. It snows heavily here.
I get out the flask for a blast of sauce.
Blonde cheerleader Debbie talking to five boys.
She squeals at the blowing snow stinging her legs,
then scrambles into a midnight-blue Oldsmobile.
The boys scrape the windshield and they drive off,
bright headlights dazzling the fresh snow.

It's no use, there's too much competition,
too many handsome guys around with Hollywood smiles,
with cunning questions and clever answers,
with easy charm and charming ease.

When I get home to Mulberry Street
I give Debbie's box of Valentine's Day candy to my mother,
to whom I've been downright hateful
for three, four, five months.

I'm sorry about my life, about girls.
I keep too many pointed breasts on my brain.

Damn them all. From now on, boy,
it's eyes in books or straight ahead.

But then there's that new brunette in Chemistry,
with calves rounder than sickle moons.

I think very hard on her in bed.
My hand works between my thighs.

PHIL DUDLEY:
Cow in the Creek

I run zigzag through apple trees,
then cut across Howard Early's farm
to watch Owl Creek fill up
with water from a summer rainstorm.
Standing in the rushing stream,
beyond the wreckage of a collapsed shed,
is a Jersey cow chewing on a pale flower.
I stare at cow; cow stares back at me.
Cow's eyes are sad and dark as plums.
Cow is wet, and she is thinking
that I'm the ghost of Johnny Appleseed?
or the lost milker of Sunflower County?
or the Lone Ranger?
Or maybe cow is thinking
she's seen me someplace before:
wading in the Kishwaukee?
boating on the Illinois?
fishing in the Fox?

Hush, you birds, quiet down.
Quit that noisy chatter.
For cow is thinking, thinking, thinking,
bamboozled in a swollen creek
full of brown rainwater,
warped boards, an old tire,
and a floating garden of torn flowers.

Go, get on home now, Ernestine.

Eva? Eleanor? Ethel?

LEWIS PERCY:
Goodbye

At last.
I've really done it.
Under a star-crazed evening sky,
I have slipped away
in an empty Burlington Northern boxcar,
which is rumbling west
toward the Mississippi River.
And like an old-time vaudeville comedian
playing the tank-town circuit,
I must ham it up:
first with my Charlie Chaplin routine,
then with a few Fred Astaire dance steps.
Now I stand erect,
my right hand over my left breast,
and I swear again to quit for good
my fumbling around
with overdue bills and Saturday night bridge,
with diapers and lawnmowers,
with iron boss and stone wife.
The lavender breath of lilacs
works deep into my lungs.
I swell like a silo in country fog.
A fresh start is what I've got,
a new place to hang a new hat.
I tell you, my friend,
there will be no sad longings for me,
no looking back.
Never.

ROWENA STARK:
  Snowman

I marveled up my snowman one more time.
But no children came.
The postman came.
The soft-water man came.
The gas man came.
They were all very kind.
My snowman lost a lot of weight.
I tried hard to be patient.
The postman left.
The soft-water man said he couldn't stay.
The gas man had to hurry off.
We waited in love's limp weather.
Just me an Charley Snowman.
But no children came.
No bright eyes anywhere.

NORBERT JOYCE:
Drummers

Yellow-lit railroad coaches
and new towns at blue dawn
run through my memories.
I had a good territory:
the Dakotas, Wisconsin,
Minnesota, and Iowa.
I kept my sample cases tidy,
was neat and courteous,
and knew my products cold.
Believe me, sonny,
they respected your old grandpa.
What did I sell? you ask.
Medicines was my line:
stuff for headaches, asthma,
stomach troubles, hay fever,
even female complaints.
I knew all the hotels,
the depots, the boardinghouses
from here to Aberdeen.
Drummers were a special breed
back in them long ago days.
''Knights of the grip''
was what they named us,
or ''commercial tourists,''
or ''trade interviewers.''
We were good at pranks,
told many a tall tale,
and were fresh as April dew
with all the country girls.
When the company went broke,
I sold cars in La Crosse,
then worked for Ward's
in Duluth and Des Moines.

But it was a real comedown:
no more good talk with friends,
no more nights in St. Paul,
and no more railroad coaches
with them yellow lights.
What's that again?
What are female complaints?
Well, boy, you see —
I think it's time for bed.

BILLY UNDERWOOD:
Memorial Day

Uncle gives his Chevy horn three sharp toots.
Mother bangs shut her new reincarnation book
and puts on rubber boots and Father's black raincoat.
The moment has come. There's no way out.

I slump in the back seat and say nothing,
a temporarily benched home run slugger
rubbing spit into the pocket of a catcher's glove.

The car starts and we're off to the graveyard.
Mother clutches two American flags from the dime store
to plant at the foot of Father's headstone.
Uncle drives slowly, tries to stay calm.

Father is only a fading memory these days,
a crabby guy who could throw a neat knuckle ball.
When I dropped a toss his scorn burned like fire.

Mother wouldn't let Father out of her sight.
Father put up with Mother as long as he could,
then left home to join the Air Corps again.
He crashed in West Berlin. Mother never cried at all.

Uncle pushes the flags into the spongy earth.
Mother raps on Father's carved stone and says,
"You won't get away with this, Howard. I won't let you."

A big grackle flies across the wet pine trees.
Mother's eyes look awful funny, real spooky.
"Let's get out of here," I say to Uncle.
"Mother is hating Father more than ever now."

GRACE RODZINSKY:
Cocktail Party

Why did I wear this dreadful dress,
the lizard-green dress with pink lace?

For the main and simple reason
you don't give me any money,
the white dress is out of season,
and I haven't any money.

Hey, I made a rhyme for you,
a little poor-wife rhyme for you,
a rhyme for you, rhyme for you.

But you say you like my hair, my face?
And you'll excuse this dowdy dress?

O lucky me. O amazing Grace.

SAM BUCKNER:
Lovers' Quarrel

At half-light I gaze at muddy water.
The brooding face of the Ausagaunaskee River
is not the face of a drowned boy
who went wading a little too far
with fishing pole or hunting dog,
nor the face of the drunk from out of town,
who fell off the railroad bridge one spring night
after losing at poker, or was it pool?
No, there are no haunting faces here,
no one to remember, no one to grieve for.
But back beyond weeping willow shadows,
a gravel road, and withered catalpa blossoms
is the face of an unhappy country girl,
wet-eyed now over a packed suitcase,
hoping to catch the next bus for Mattoon
so she can tell Mama and Papa
about the mean mouth she got married to.

ESTELLE ETHEREGE:
Fifty

Today I am 50 years old. 50!

Coming up the hill from the meat market,
I can see that my house is in sad shape.
The front porch sags, a window is broken,
and the wind chips off flakes of paint.

51, 52, 53, 54, 55, 56...70!

HEIDI KOENIG:
Slow Day at the Office

The raindrop
on the right
would have
overtaken
the raindrop
on the left
in the match race
down my
windowpane
but
the raindrop
on the right
ran smack into
the blood bug
of the week
so
the raindrop
on the left
won
easily
and that's
when
the big boss said
"Heidi!"

WILBURN MILLER:
Tough Guy

In grade school
the teachers
they always called me
Wilburn.
And as I look back
to them days,
that could have been
the reason
right there
why I hated the place
so awful much,
why I knifed up
every desk I sat behind
and wouldn't never
say a single word
to nobody
nor read from a book
or put numbers
up on the blackboard.
Because my name
is Bud.
Bud is my only name.
Just Bud.
And no one
in the poolroom
or on the section gang
dares to call me
Wilburn,
because they know
damn well
I would swear
something terrible
and scratch and bite.
So does this
keep me out
of the Army,
doctor?

SELMA SKOGLAND:
Peanut Butter

When Marty came home from the Marines,
after getting a dishonorable discharge,
he lost no time in telling us
that he was going away to become a hairdresser.
Dad merely shrugged, grunted twice,
and went right on reading the night ball scores.

Then Jack joined the Salvation Army
and wrote that he was content for once,
working up a righteous sweat on a bass drum
and saving souls on street corners.
Dad didn't even grunt this time.
He only coughed and blew his nose.

But no goofy sons were about to outdo Dad.
When it came to being nuts, he was the whole tree.
In fact, just yesterday he took off for Mexico,
taking the family's red Edsel,
eleven jars of Peter Pan peanut butter,
and the plumber's teenage wife.

DOUG CHANDLER:
Television

I have decided, Doris,
that it's time to stand up tall
and let you have it flat out.
Until you get yourself a TV set,
I'll not sit any more nights
on your electric-blue rayon plush couch.
Do you understand, Doris?
I'm missing too many exciting shows,
too many athletic thrills.
Also, the act we put on
night after night after night
will never be a big hit.

GUY HANSEN:
Retirement

I quit my stool at the Spot-Lite Diner,
a toothpick jumping between my teeth,
then moving over to the steamy window
I watch the long, quiet rain.

Standing here, cracked hands unclosing, closing,
wearing a blue sweat-faded work shirt,
my laboring man's body grows tense, twitches,
the noon factory whistle blowing shrilly.

I think: *So this is retirement, this empty nothing?*
And feeling cheated, the angry thoughts come:
no wife, no children, no more work to do,
forty years a millwright now drained away.

I step out into Sixth Street muttering to myself,
not noticing the cold, persistent rainsoak,
fears of uselessness and numbing boredom
screaming along the assembly line of my brain.

Turning to duck under a sheltered doorway
to relight a Marsh Wheeling cigar,
my throat is dry as sawdust,
the match flaring, burning down, winking out.

BETSY PETTIGREW:
Carnival on Eye Street

The two-bit,
three-day carnival
they have every August
in this one-horse town
is set up again
on the same weedy lot
at the end of Eye Street.
And we are going
to the carnival,
as we always do,
but not for the fun of it,
not to eat cotton candy,
not to shoot metal ducks,
not to see the tractor pull,
and most certainly
not to ride the merry-go-round.
No, we keep going back
year after year
to win us a new car.
And this year
we got six tickets
on a Ford Thunderbird,
and if we win,
Pappy says
I can learn to drive,
if I don't think sixty
is too old to learn how.

LUANNE ELLIOTT:
Escaping the Holy Rollers

The wind smelled of wet leather.
I wanted summer rain to gallop me down
in a field of flowering weeds.

A squall line was building up in the west.
I heard hooves pound beyond the sun,
drumming across the long flanks of sky.

Two lathered men had come to the house,
burdened with booklets about Jesus.
When they knocked, I could not answer.

Instead, I ran to that high place
in back of the town water tower,
desperate for space and fresh air.

Lightning came and thunder came,
but no rain followed the saddled wind.
I remained dry as Noah's ark.

Later on I pulled up carrots
by the light of an oat-straw moon,
then slept, dreaming of wild-eyed horses.

MACK SCARCE:
Going Steady

A mad, moon-soaked, May midnight.
I'm walking home past darkened houses.

This wormy shortcut through tall weeds.
My skin is damp with passion sweat.

Pale gold flesh of her plump thighs.
The brown curly hair of her sex.

She tickles, she squeezes, she fondles.
She drives me crazy with kisses.

Think: marry her? or not marry her?
Wild plum drops a white blossom.

Tall brick chimney at Franklin School.
It sticks up like a proud penis.

RUBY KIMBLE:
Homecoming Game

My poor sister Patsy
had a fly go in her mouth
when she was singing
"The Star-Spangled Banner"
at the homecoming game
over to Champaign.

No, it didn't come out.
She must of swallowed it.
She said it flew in after
she went past the words,
"what so proudly we hailed,"
or some such like that.

She kept her mouth shut
for the entire game.
Didn't even cheer when
Illinois scored a touchdown.
No, I don't know who won.
Buy yourself a paper.

HARLAN ADCOCK:
Body

The dead man in my October cornfield
should have run off quick to Switzerland,
is not in shape to hunt pheasants,
lies on his side, his hands tied,
wears cuff links the size of door knockers,
has frosty-morning whiskers, rusty teeth,
won't do for fertilizer,
can't pull up his socks or tuck in his shirt,
looks a good bit like Pretty Boy Floyd,
doesn't hear the caw of crows,
will miss the Army-Navy game,
could be a gangster from Chicago,
was shot once in the head, twice in the heart.

OWEN HENDERSON:
Bad Night on Blue Hollow Road

What happened was
was that I blew a left front tire last night
way out on Blue Hollow Road,
about a half mile or so off Illinois 64,
and I'm getting out the tools
and looking around for the Eveready lantern
when a load of doped-up kids pull up
and start to make fun of my trouble.

What happened was
was that they all pile out of the car,
six or maybe even eight of them there were,
including this one puny bit of a girl
taking little noisy sips from a can of beer,
and they commence to push and shove each other,
wanting to work the jack,
and then the tall guy hurts his hand.

What happened was
was that the fat guy gets sore at the girl,
saying she was showing me her underwear,
and the guy with the bad limp
works me over with an ugly brown bottle,
and laying there in the weedy ditch,
I hear them drive off, yelling and cursing,
the road dust drifting across my bloody face.

DONALD GUEST:
Boredom

She hardly ever leaves the house anymore,
what with cooking the meals,
washing the clothes, scrubbing the floors.
But during the past year or so
she's enjoyed some real good-time afternoons
over at the Congregational church,
gabbing and giggling with the Gaston sisters
and gluing covers back on hymnbooks.

She says I'm bored because I'm boring.
I say I'm bored because she's boring.

She hates my left-wing politics, my goatee,
my choice collection of Japanese prints.

What she does like is cream style corn
and bowling on television.

Listen here, funny Florence has had her fun.
Now, by God, I want mine.

KELSEY JUDD:
Murder

Evenings, when the heat of the day is past,
an eerie orange light burns on the porch
and people stroll by and say,
"That's where it happened, that's the place.
She's dead, she's dead and gone,
and the kids are in the orphanage
asking when their ma is coming back."
Everyone in town knows about it now,
that some crazy man stabbed her six times,
after locking both little girls in the bedroom.
Everyone knows that the cops
are soon to solve the crime.
Everyone knows that for a fact, all right.
But this is what they don't know:
that I picked her up outside a roadside bar
and drove her home for drinks and kisses,
just four weeks ago tonight.
Everyone knows the house is up for sale
and her car was sold for junk.
But only I know about the green shorts
I stripped off her slender body
and stashed inside my shirt.
Though I've tried awfully hard of late
to be nice and natural with folks,
it seems I can't get along with anyone anymore.
What I am is a right shoe on a left foot,
a flat tire on a mountain road,
the last match in a howling wind.
I sit by the cat thinking about that
and wait for the knock on my kitchen door.

LINDA FULGHAM:
Ida May and Ida May Not

There's a man sitting on an orange bench
my aunt Ida would sure like to meet.
She's been painting all day and all night.
She put him on that orange bench, you see.
In Ida's painting of man and bench,
the man sits closer to Auntie than
she knows he would if he had a choice.
Yet she has painted herself right there,
kneeling in the sparse grass at his feet.
She is going crazy painting men,
needing men, wanting men she can't have.
It's just too bad the way things go wrong.
Nobody seems to know what to do.
The funny farm is waiting close by.
Will Aunt Ida make it through the night?
Well, Ida may and Ida may not.

VELMA WITHERSPOON:
Mischief

"It's raining, so what's there to do?"
When my brother says that,
you'd better watch out, that's for sure.
He gets that devilish look in his eyes,
and you can't laugh him into temperance
or calm him with milk and cookies.
When he's bored he turns into big trouble.
He's not the same person at all,
any more than Clark Kent is
after he changes clothes in a phone booth.
We've been through things, Mother and I.
We've been through ink, paint, nails,
floor polish, gasoline, and tar.
And thank the good Lord that Father
has locked up Al's BB gun.
Don't worry, we'll keep our eyes on him
this rainy April afternoon.
Even our dog Pinky is wide awake.
She never has gotten over the shock
of being the first green poodle in town.

BRADFORD TULLEY:
Lonesome

Lonely? No, not lonely.
Lonesome! Lonesome, as in
"look down that lonesome road."
I'm a Corn Belt farmer's son,
in case you have forgotten that.
Here in the Middle West,
one can grow very lonesome,
which goes beyond just plain lonely.
Lonesome! Do you hear me?
And today I was gosh-awful lonesome,
looking at the bare trees,
the bleak houses, the bland barns,
the oh so empty fields.
You aren't around anymore
to take a little piece of the lonesome
out of my old December.
I'll bet you're not sorry, either.
You don't know what lonely is,
let alone lonesome.
Now that you're in the big city,
you probably don't care a bit
for the boy you left behind
on a corn and cow farm
in cold-lonesome Sunflower County.
Darn you, Caroline,
you won't even write.

HOLLY JO ANDERSON:
Bein' Poor

We live in a too confinin' trailer
with two busted clocks,
a cracked mirror, and no maw.

Our paw is out of work agin.
He has a little drinkin' problem
and his ears don't match.

Flodeen greets all trains,
all Greyhound buses,
and winks at good lookin' strangers.

DeWayne draws naked ladies,
fools with mice and matches,
and picks scabs at church meetin'.

Me? Oh, I do what I can do:
darnin' socks, stealin' fruit,
helpin' Paw get his clothes off.

We don't like it bein' poor.
But things they start out bad
and they just stay bad.

Last year we was in Taylorville.
This year it's Alliance.
Nobody's tellin' 'bout next year.

WESLEY HARKNESS:
Why He Didn't Repair the Bookcase

I tried.
Right after school.
I couldn't do it.
The wood splits.
Damn nails.
Guess they're just too big.
Or I'm clumsy.
I tried.
Here's your hammer.
It hits pretty good.
Damn nails.
Hate antiques.
Nothing but old junk.
Do it yourself.
I tried.

RAYMOND KAFARSKI:
Wheels

My rusty-dusty
blue Toyota,
deep in Zen prayer
under the willow tree,
is looking more and more
ornamental
as the years roll past.
It's been some seven years
since I took it
or it took me
out to Oregon
to see Aunt Becky,
sweating all the way,
trying to stay clear
of the big diesel trucks,
feeling like a midget
in Mammothville.
It's shot to hell now.
If I don't junk it
pretty damn quick,
it won't be too long
before some wise guy
or solemn ass
stops his new Corvette,
LeMans, Cutlass,
or Monte Carlo
and comments with a smile,
"Say, nice bait bucket
you got there, mister.
You oughta plant
some pink petunias
in that old thing
and pretty-up the yard."

SALLY WHIPPLE:
    Great-Grandmother's Speech on New Year's Eve

I didn't say I wasn't going.
I said maybe I won't be going.
But a party's a party,
so to go is to keep going.
And I aim to keep going.

Old man, get me my shoes.

PETER VOSBURGH:
Return to River Street

That's the place, 12 River Street, our old house,
and your tire is still hanging from the maple tree.
Let's get out of the car, shall we, son?
We'll stand on the sidewalk and have us a look.
Your mother would go right up and ring the bell,
but I don't want to bother them for an inside tour.
Up there where the shades are pulled was your room.
Do you remember the Lionel train you played with?
The track went all around, even under your bed.
I can't believe we've been gone for five years.
Kansas City is okay and the job is going fine,
though you're not as happy as I'd have you, my boy.
You were a real Tom Sawyer or Huck Finn here,
the Ausagaunaskee River being just down the bank.
Maybe it was wrong to move, to leave this town.
Some men can be led astray and not even know it.
You'd better not swing on the tire, son.
Come on, get off, it's not yours to fool with now.
Oh, well, go ahead and have yourself some fun,
then let's get a cold pop and get back on the road.

IRMA GILLESPIE:
Chicken Bone

This morning I found a chicken bone
under my bed, if you can beat that.
The damn cat got in the garbage again.
No wonder I dreamed of you and me,
hand in hand, oh so lovey-dovey,
at the annual Elks picnic,
in the summer of 1964.
Then romantic 1964
slipped off into 1965,
and when the next picnic came around,
you were there, but with someone else.
I watched you win the three-legged race,
wishing it were our legs tied together.
Damn cat, dragging picnic-love dreams
into my dreaming, single-bed room.
And damn you, Danny, for coming back,
if only in a silly dream of mine.
After you left the county for keeps,
I thought I had you junked for good,
dropped in a bag with other scraps
and put out on the Monday curb
for the garbage truck to haul away.
Of course when you were living here
you knew I had a crush on you.
In September 1963,
you said, obviously amused,
"Who is that strange girl behind the oak tree?
She follows me wherever I go."

TOOKIE THORNHILL:
Cleaning Up the Yard

We had a huge windstorm most of last night.
It was hard for me and Teddy to sleep.
Mom said she didn't get a single wink.
We all went outside and looked at branches.
The wind broke branches off every tree.
"Well, there's our firewood for next fall," Mom said.
Daddy and Teddy they just shook their heads.
"We got heaps of hard work to do," I said.
"You best stay away, Tookie," Teddy said.
Daddy got out his saw with the sharp teeth.
"I'll do the sawing," he said to Teddy.
I made a pile of the fattest fat leaves.
I carried seventeen leaves to the curb.
Teddy said I wasn't helping any.
Daddy said I was too helping any.
There were leaves, leaves, leaves all over the grass.
It took me tons of ages to pile them.
Daddy sawed those big branches up real good.
"Let me saw for awhile now," Teddy said.
Daddy said no and brushed Teddy away.
My work began when my fun was not fun.
It was tempting to quit and play with dolls.
But I wanted to piss with the big dogs.
That's something I heard Daddy say one time.
He said it to Mr. Willis next door.
Mom doesn't like that kind of talk one bit.
Piss is one naughty word she won't stand for.
Daddy made dozens of little branches.
"Okay, let's stack these nice and neat," he said.
"If I can't saw, I won't work," Teddy said.
"Tookie, you come help me, then," Daddy said.
"Piss," I said to Daddy, "piss, piss, piss, piss."
And then I ran down the street with Teddy.

SYLVESTER F. BILLINGS:
The Civil War

Jess, when you fell on that icy playground
and broke your leg in three places
they took you to Alliance Community Hospital,
and when they let you out
you were wearing a big white cast
on which all of your school chums
wrote their names and get-well messages,
and you could not play basketball anymore,
nor skate on the pond with Rhoda Collins,
and so you moped around the house for awhile
until you finally settled down with a book
and started reading about Abe Lincoln and Jeff Davis
and General Sherman and General Grant
and about the Army of the Cumberland
and the Army of Northern Virginia
and about the Battle of Missionary Ridge
and the siege of Vicksburg
and about the 2nd Iowa and the 52nd Illinois
and Andersonville and Appomattox,
and before we knew it
there was another Civil War buff
in the Sylvester F. Billings family,
and that suits us just fine,
because from now on, my son,
when we speak of The War under this roof
you will know full well
of which war we are talking about.

EMMYLOU OBERKFELL:
Fifth Grade Poem on America

America
is
a big
Christmas
pie:
the Middle West
is berries,
the rest
is
just
crust.

LLOYD KELLOGG:
The Man Who Played Clarinet in the High School Band Back in 1936, But Then Never Amounted to Anything Much After That, Is Here Again Today, Folks

I'm rooted to this curbstone.
I won't vamoose, won't leave from here,
though my soaked shoes grow sloppy
and my shirt sticks like a stamp.
The Fourth of July. American flags.
It's a parade is what I'm waiting on.
Hey, look there, here it comes now!
My old excitement is coming too,
because right down Illinois Street
the band, the high school band,
with blare of brass, crash of drums,
is stepping off smartly in the rain.
There I am. That's me. Right there.
See my snazzy clarinet?
Yes, sir, I'm a real proud one today.
I'm really strutting my stuff
before two dozen relatives
just in from Jericho Corners.
Lord, "The Washington Post" march!
We did that one. We did it good.
Now the music is fading, fading away.
I can no longer hear my clarinet.
Well, it's over again, yes, again.
And too soon, much too soon,
forgotten me will disappear
under wet maple leaves,
trampled by an oom-pah tuba player.
I could just almost cry.
I walk slowly up Illinois Street.
I don't feel like doing nothing.

KATHY SCHOONOVER:
Identity

For supper last night,
I was opening a can
of Joan of Arc kidney beans,
staring at the can
as it turned round and round and round.
"Mother," I said.
"Yes, dear," she said.
"I'm not what you think I am,
not what you hope I am,
because what I am
is someone I don't know I am."
"How's that again?" she said.
"Oh, Mother!" I said.
"Did I say something wrong?" she said.
"Oh, Mother!" I said.
I left the can on the stove
and marched out of the room.
Later, I had to laugh.
Joan of Arc kidney beans?
Now there's one for the book.

GREGORY DAWSON:
Sick Before Supper

What they did was to serve bad booze,
the cheap bourbon, the bargain gin.
Anyway, when it came time to eat,
only three of us could get there
to dine on shrimp cocktails and big T-bone steaks.
Neil was on his knees by the toilet bowl.
Peter and Sharon were out by the pump.
Carla was lying down on the couch,
moaning about strange tasting hors d'oeuvres.
But it wasn't the food, nothing we ate.
It was the cut-rate hooch that did us dirt.
We drank too much of it, of course.
It was that kind of party, that kind of group.
Some folks don't mix with some folks, that's all.
Now if I can just stop being sick,
here in the yard, bending over a tall weed,
I'm going to go straight on home
and pour myself a decent scotch.

RUSSELL HAYES:
Federal Highway

"Gone," he said.
"What's gone?" I said.
"It won't never be the same," he said.
"What won't never?" I said.
"The farm, the farm," he said.
"My god, what's gone wrong?" I said.
"They ran a federal highway through it," he said.
"Then gone is what it is," I said.
"Oh, it's still there," he said.
"But you aren't there," I said.
"That's right," he said.
"It's just not no place to farm now," I said.
"No, it ain't," he said.
"Then you're gone for good?" I said.
"Gone," he said.

KERMIT OLMSTED:
Roots

"We're staying right here the rest of our lives," I said.
"In Illinois?" she said.
"That's where we are, isn't it?" I said.

MILDRED CESAREK:
At the Crossroads

I sit in the kitchen and wind my watch.

Above this crossroads store
Grandma can't fry eggs anymore.

She's buried in a graveyard box,
north wind blowing around her name,
a shovel propped against a tilted stone.

Sleet rattles in the withered corn.

Lying upside down on a pink platter of pins
is Grandma's silly looking Easter hat.
Because Suzy cries when she sees it now,
I hide it in the cellar behind the onion sack.

Pine trees are stiff with thick ice.

There have been too many griefs here,
too many ghosts whose graves I know,
too many eyes that stare at mine.

Above this crossroads store
Grandma can't crochet anymore.

I will mourn her best I can.

LAMAR WOCKENFUSS:
Friendly Persuasion

The damp corn silk
sticking out
of this ear of sweet corn
is the pubic hair
of my blonde girl friend,
who just asked,
while running her hand
under my gold shorts,
if we could go
to the movies tonight
and did I have
enough money
for hot buttered popcorn?

CALVIN FAIRBANKS:
Letter to Grandma

Mother says
I haven't
written you
in five years
but I never
had nothing to say
until
now
that is
and I'm just busting
to tell you
we saw
Adolph Hitler's
personal
armored
bullet-proof
car.

We were over
to the fair
and there it was
and was I surprised
I didn't
expect
nothing
like that
to turn up
among all those
pigs and pickles
Jimmy didn't
neither
wow-eeee
how are you Gram
love
Cal.

HELEN ALBRIGHT:
Booster

What you mean why I grow these sunflowers?
This is Sunflower County, isn't it?
Why folks all the time ask silly questions?

I'll pass out my sunflowers on Main Street.
I'll send sunflowers to Salt Lake City.

Sunflowers, I'm talking up sunflowers.

PORTER KNOX:
  The Christmas Tree

Above Sam Kuykendall's dime store a loudspeaker blares
a never-ending selection of Christmas carols.

O little town of Bethlehem
How still we see thee lie,
Above thy deep and dreamless sleep
The silent stars go by.

Years ago, when I was the head of a large family,
before everyone either died or moved away for good,
we always had a brightly-lit scotch pine or balsam fir
at Christmastime on the farm near Noon Prairie.
I remember the avalanche of presents, the happy faces,
the huge turkey dinners with candlelight and wine.

I shouldn't have done it, I guess, but I did it.
I went out into the teeth of a zero-cold wind,
walked up to the Christmas tree man at the A&P,
stamped my freezing feet in the icy parking lot,
and demanded to buy the biggest tree for sale,
having found thirty dollars in the tobacco-tin bank.
Oh, I had to have a Christmas tree on Christmas Eve,
and I was willing to leave a sick bed to get one,
willing to drag it back to my room on Illinois Street.

I will have to string popcorn to decorate my tree.
I have neither time nor strength to search for lights
or red and green balls or the soiled blue angel.
My old man's hands flutter like wounded quail.
I puff my pipe, cough, then slump to the floor.
A newspaper catches fire and the popcorn and the tree.

Still in thy dark night shineth
The everlasting light,
The hopes and fears of all the years
Are met in thee tonight.

The fire engine screams through the tinseled streets.
Now no one can hear "Silent Night, Holy Night."

MOE OTT:
Deathbed Words of a Life Insurance Salesman

The boss said,
"You must
sell yourself,
my boy."

So I did,
and soon
sold myself
for life.

ELMER PRATT:
Revelation

Though she quailed from me,
by dribbles and drabbles I wormed
the cold truth out of her.

She had sinned, and by God
there would be redemption or I
was no Christian father at all.

The nerve of her telling us
that she was going to a school play,
then going instead to a gin mill!

Her story was very roundabout, but
I could smell the booze,
knew male hands had crawled her flesh.

I took off my leather belt,
pulled her panties below her knees,
and let her have it good.

Though she wailed and pled,
I could not stop smacking those
white and plump and lovely buns.

The more my passion grew,
the more confused I got.
Then she wrenched away from me.

Oh, how quickly it comes upon you
that your child is no longer child
but a woman, woman fleshed.

KAREN HICKS:
  Loony

That
woman
there
who
could
be
and
maybe
is
my
ancient
and
loony
aunt
from
Ko-
ko-
mo
rises
up
from
her
garden
in
bright
purple
shoes
and
bites
a
big
sun-
flower.

CURTIS LURTSEMA:
National Pastime

Baseball is a game I know something about, boy.
I've played ball for forty years or more:
with a truck driver who hated trucks,
with my grandpa of the Dizzy Dean chatter,
with a Canadian who swore in Spanish,
with a glue-sniffer from New Glarus, Wisconsin,
with a fatso who always fell down,
with a thirteen-year-old Vietnamese kid,
with a prostitute named Eva,
with my uncle Barney of the busted bat,
with a conductor off the Rock Island Lines,
with a hotshot fertilizer salesman,
with a semipro who lived over the grocery store,
with a 200-pound lady wrestler,
with a dwarf who came to town with the circus,
with a farmer's daughter out of Fayette County,
with a bozo who once met Vince DiMaggio,
with my dad of the roundhouse curve,
with a steam fitter who would rather drink gin,
with a one-eyed guy with no eyebrows,
with a friend who wore a Phillies cap,
with a beanpole who starred for Bradley U,
with a girl I got married to,
with my brother of the head-first slide,
with a cop who swiped my catcher's mitt.
I've played ball in April rain and August heat.
I've played with snow on the ground
and when fall leaves blew across second base.
Hey, it's good news you got yourself a glove.
We will have to toss a few after lunch.
Or right now, if you can wait to eat.

REGINA WASHINGTON:
Incompatibility

After working all morning long in my
sad-rag and mop-flop kitchen,
I said to myself, I said, "Woman,
you've got to lie down
before you just plain fall down."
So on the daybed in the dining room
I stretched out on the spread.
Outside, the squirrels
ran up the tree trunks
and the tall weeds grew taller.
I must have slept at least an hour,
and when I awoke I knew
the awful, terrible truth,
the painful, headline truth.
I knew I'd rather look
at a sink full of dirty dishes
than look at him, my husband.
When I tell Norman the news,
I'll say "in-com-pat-i-bil-i-ty."
What I won't say is that
during my afternoon nap
on the daybed of housewife dreams
I heard the weeds say his name
and saw the flying feet of squirrels
dig into my broom-tired bones.

MAYBELLE JONES:
A Trip to the Bank

It was the very yesterday.
We went to town again.

The bank had a cold bench.
My legs giggled me silly.

Mama whispered her mouth.
Spitty Baby grabbed tight.

We both had wet panties on.
I felt like an oyster, you know.

The man was full of money.
''Nice to meet you,'' I said.

Mama clicked her mushy purse.
We left with our smiles going.

A big sun wrinkled my eyes.
Squirrels told naughty secrets.

Home was good to see.
But I forgot my beaded bag.

Mama said it wasn't funny.
Spitty Baby got spanked too.

Walks are nothing fun.
Now don't talk me into that.

GLORIA HAWTHORNE:
Her Dying Child

River is choked with sand.
Stacy limps down Pine Street.
This sun-baked September.
Crop duster dusting crops.
That cat, that tree, that stone.
She loves what she can touch.
Wine from the vine is mine.
Old bumbling bumblebee.
Stacy sprawls on pale grass.
My heart hums a slow tune.

KATE PINCHOT:
  Public Library

Books, books, books, books, books, books.
A dark, nasty Wednesday library night.
Tarkington, Thackeray, Tolstoy.
Big splash of rain against high windows.
"Yes, Mr. Roodhouse, we've had too much rain."
Stacks of books to put away again.
Galsworthy, Glasgow, Graham Greene.
Kid in farm cap asks about Mickey Spillane.
Crumpled library card I can't read.
Awful old man asleep over his *Fortune.*
Wet copy of *The Tin Drum* falls off the desk.
"Overdue means just that: overdue."
Three teenage girls giggle near the rubber plant.
"I'll accept the stamp but not bubble gum."
James Joyce, Henry James, James Jones.
The magazine racks are a mess.
Table heaped with Cracker Jack boxes.
These kids come here to eat, not study.
Two smashed Milk Duds sink into the carpet.
Would sure love to swat that Rukenbrod boy.
Wendy Witherspoon is no angel, either.
"Five minutes to closing time, five minutes."
Books on anatomy, biology, chess.
Books on falconry, gourmet cooking, health.
"No, mam, George Eliot is not a man.
Neither is Joyce Kilmer a woman.
Well, it's not *my* fault, Mrs. Mott."
Baudelaire, Verlaine, Rimbaud.
Another complaint from right-wing nincompoop.
"Yes, *The Grapes of Wrath* is a great book."
Must wake up that old man real quick.
"Okay, that's it, everyone must go, at once."
New novels scream in their bright jackets.
The big dictionary chokes on its forgotten words.

Masters and Lewis sob on the back shelf.
Civil War books hum old battle songs.
Louisa May Alcott lays down and dies.
Lightning, thunder, pelting rain.
"Leave that magazine here, please."
Oh God, let me lock the door and get out, now.
This librarian is drowning in books.
Books, books, books, books, books, books.

LEONARD MASSINGAIL:
Fatherly Advice

You don't know beans about girls
and you are going about half-cocked.
It will always be a wild-goose chase
until, by hook or crook,
you break the ice with her.
She'll let you cool your heels
as long as you beat about the bush.
It's no skin off my nose
if you can't cut the mustard
and act like a fish out of water.
I'm not talking through my hat
when I say you're asleep at the switch.
Getting a doll is no lead-pipe cinch,
and coming down with a case of cold feet
puts romance on the rocks.
She sure looks like the real McCoy,
so make hay while the sun shines.
Get yourself in the groove, son.
Go the whole hog, right now.
I'd sweat my good blood
to rule the roost with that chick.
Just be a chip off the old block
and you'll soon be on Easy Street.
If you're going to hem and haw,
I'm going to be madder than a wet hen.
Look, either fish or cut bait,
or you will always eat crow.
Damnit, take the bull by the horns!

JACK ERTEL:
The Fighter

Nubs Lilly liked to use his fists.
A while back, during an overheated discussion
at our Saturday night poker session,
he, as usual, got in the first punch.
But it was also his last one,
because this gas-pump jockey named Jolly,
from over in Kendall County,
quickly laid him out with a nifty left hook.
Later, Nubs had to admit
that he had had enough of the fight game
and was not really another up-and-coming
"Two Ton Tony" Galento.

Now it's worse, for he's lifting weights
and talking all the time about Frank Gotch,
Hackenschmidt, and Stanislaus Zbyszco.
He fancies himself a wrestler, you see,
and all his cronies have grown very tired
of being asked to "go a fall or two."
Phil Graham says that if Nubs
keeps on flapping his big yap,
he's going to toss his ass into Park Street.
When I tell Nubs this latest bit of news,
he gives me a slow smile and says,
"Strangler Lilly spits on that kind of talk."

DAWN CASAGRANDE:
Concert

Until the cops came
and took him away,
there was a bearded stranger
in a black-and-white-checked suit
playing the harmonica
on the sidewalk in front
of our defunct opera house.
He had attracted a small crowd
of Saturday shoppers
and a few old men
who wandered over
from the clean green benches
on the Courthouse lawn.
The cops were gentle but firm.
No one said anything
in the way of protest,
except lame Johnny Johncock,
who asked if the man
could maybe stick around
a wee bit longer
so he could play his
''Roses of Picardy'' again.

ARNOLD WHEELER:
Ambition

The big white house on Harvester Street.
Back home again for another Christmas.
We sit before a feisty log fire.
Pyramids of presents, boxes, wrapping paper.
Talk of what he got, what she got.
Brag of what money can buy.
Then they turn their tongues on me.
"What do you study at college?" Father says.
"Gauguin and Van Gogh," I say.
"What is your favorite subject?" Mother says.
"Modigliani," I say.
"Just what *do* you get out of school?" Father says.
"How to draw the nude," I say.

"What do you want to be?" Father says.
"See that maple tree over there?" I say.
"Yes, I see it. So what?" Father says.
"Well, that's what I want to be," I say.
"Trees don't do a damn thing," Father says.
"Now you've got the idea, Pop," I say.

"I just want to loaf and invite my soul," I say.
"What's this rubbish about a soul?" Father says.
"It never comes up in the gas business," I say.

By the time another Christmas comes calling,
I'm living in a cold rented room,
two thousand miles from cozy home and hearth.
"How come a bright fellow like you
is working nights loading trucks?"
my landlady says, dialing down the heat,
reaching for another sweater.
"Why don't you show more ambition?"
"Andy Warhol," I inform her,
hoping she will change the subject.

BRIAN HARDY:
Little Theater

They were casting
for William Inge's
Picnic tonight.
I went right over
and said I wanted
to be Hal Carter,
the guy who comes
to this Kansas town
and makes all the girls
go crazy with lust.
I told them
Picnic was my
favorite stage play
and I knew all the words
Hal Carter has to say
and that I was
just like Hal Carter.
They looked me
up and down
and shook their heads,
and I saw a smile
on the director's face.
He said, "Young man,
you're a bit too short
to play Hal.
Not husky enough.
Not enough big white teeth."
They told me
I could try out
for another role,
but I told them no.
I was Hal Carter
or nothing at all.

They said, "We're sorry.
We're awful sorry."
I left the theater
and walked out
into a pouring rain,
knowing I was stuck
with being me
for a while longer.
I stopped for milk
and a cheeseburger
at the Spot-Lite Diner.
There was this girl
I like real good there.
I told her, "Holly,
you think you're hot stuff,
but you're not."
She was hurt and I'm glad.
William Inge, you can
write this down too:
"Life ain't no picnic
for Brian Hardy."

JONI LEFEVRE:
Bicycle Ride to the Cannery

Hot, hot, hot morning. Hate like shit to steam up so
quick. Worm-slimy sun. Knees pumping. Old wreck of a beat
bicycle. Face sweaty. Sticky thighs. Swimming is
where I want to be. Maybe nude at Potter's Pond.
Bobby equals sex. Ronald equals skinny prick.
Like big everything. Damn pothole. Fuck truck. Must cut
my long hair. Strip. Cold shower. Massage my rubber-hard
nipples. Bigger than Beverly's. Roger's stiff cock
when he walked away. Milo's muscles. Curly weeds.
Pubic itch. Cannery again. One more all-day
date with peas and beans. Oh hell's burnt carrots. I want
icy drinks. Bare feet. Windchimes on a shady porch. Not
this devil's trip to a summer-rotting jail. Crap.

GOLDIE KLIPSTEIN:
Creative Writing

My boy will never
know higher mathematics
or mechanical engineering,
and there's no Harvard
in his future, either,
no job making big money
in Houston
or Los Angeles,
for when I found
''Between two red barns,
corn stubble sticking up
above the snow:
ragged yellow candles
on a giant's
birthday cake''
typed on bond paper
and later printed
in the new *Catalpa Review,*
I knew he was a poet,
and thanked God
his father wasn't around
to see his only son
plunging wide-eyed
into creative writing.

MICKEY CONWAY:
Tornado Warning

Tornado warning!
I snatch my shoe box of gum-dusty
bubble gum baseball cards
and hightail it to the cellar.
"What's so awful special
about those baseball cards?"
says my sister, pouting,
hugging a couple of overdressed dolls.
Mom fills three jelly glasses
with Country Time lemonade.
"Look here," I say,
"if the house blows down
with all our furniture and stuff,
I can start a new house with
Smoky Burgess and Ewell Blackwell,
Wally Post and Vada Pinson,
Harvey Haddix and Solly Hemus,
Curt Flood and Roy Face,
Mickey Vernon and Elmer Valo,
Eddie Joost and Larry Jackson,
Johnny Logan and Whitey Lockman."
My sister gives me a sour look.
Mom smiles, squeezes my arm.
I open the shoe box
and take out Richie Ashburn, who had
a lifetime batting average of .308.
"Not bad," I say, "not bad at all."
"Drink your lemonade," Mom says.
"Yeah, drink your lemonade,"
says my sister, putting shoes
on a prune-face doll.
This is the third time this month
we've been down here
with the sack of peat moss,
the busted-up croquet set,
and two years of old newspapers.
I want to tell you something.
I'm getting a bit tired of hearing
"tornado warning!"

NANCY EASTWICK:
Jericho Township

No one tells me where I was born.
Look, hawk shadow across white barn.
Pain of loss, pain of being lost.
Quick goodbye after sweat of lust.
Dying rabbit bleeds in blood dust.
Blue tractor cools off at blue dusk.
I want a tall horse, a gold coin.
Now who calls my name from fall corn?

HAMILTON RIVERS:
Noon at Carl's Mainline Cafe

Talk of septic tanks, sheep dip, soap powder.
Talk just to be talking, saying something:

"Claude says the water is more than four feet deep
in those corn bottoms south the highway bridge."

"I'm gonna sell my galvanized hay loader,
my metal detector, and my Star Wars bedspread."

"You say he's a duck decoy carver now
and you haven't seen him since last Arbor Day?"

"Joe Webb dropped dead after this evangelist fella
got him over excited and puking his guts."

"I sure guess it needs a new transmission, boy.
Why you can't even back that heap up anymore."

"He's a loud kid in Big Smith overalls.
Fergus is his name, and it fits him to a T."

"Kay don't care much for her Kenmore washing machine.
Says never again another product from Sears."

"We cleaned out all that junk in the attic.
All them boxes with your forgotten toys in them."

"Funny thing, the area code here is 312.
Yet right across my street it's 815."

"Me and Willie we used to get us free wienies
from Rukenbrod's store when we'd stop from school."

"I unwrapped it and it was waxed fruit.
Sister ain't had no sense since she gone to Tulsa."

"Leave me inform you them wienies were good.
Seems they was better tasting than cooked ones."

"If I want to talk with Mabel Anderson,
I'm required to dial for long distance."

"It wasn't junk, it wasn't junk at all.
That was my Lionel train in there, you idiot."

"Ma's got herself an old Maytag, you know.
Pa he bought a platform rocker the very same day."

"Young Fergus is a pretty fair country jock,
but he bumbles about without benefit of brains."

"You was talkin' on rusty cars what leak.
We drove up here with water sloshing in the trunk."

"Ain't it sumpthing to go to your grave like that.
And Joe he never had a girl in bed or nothin'."

"I dropped Cousin Daisy a card from Vero Beach.
It comes back stamped RETURNED TO SENDER."

"What I need is a double-oven electric range
and maybe some new oars for the rowboat."

"Well, that's our flood for this April.
That's about per usual for Sunflower County."

Damn, I wish I hadn't heard all that nonsense.
I don't even remember what the hell I ate.

WAYNE V. NOYES, JR.:
Front Porch Swing

The old custom
of sitting
on the cozy
front porch swing
on a summer night
when dusk
smells like warm
clover grass
is not one
to tamper with,
for when else does
a big pipe load
of Carter Hall
go so well
right after
a huge bowl
of strawberry
ice cream
and a ripe peach?

And maybe
close neighbors
with cold beer
and a banjo
will walk up
under the drooping
sycamore leaves,
mosquitoes
stabbing
their sweaty
arms and necks,
and we will
sing and swing
way beyond
the ten o'clock
news of the world,
and who cares
if the rusty
chains creak?

ROSE GARABALDI:
Real Estate

It was last year I gave up
any notion of becoming
the biggest woman in real estate
in all of northern Illinois,
Wisconsin, and half of Canada,
and so went on a starvation diet,
taking off almost 200 pounds.
Now when I go to work
I step outside in my featherweight body
and wait for a west wind
to float me like goose down
right through the open door
of Gust Reinhart Realty.
Oh, it's been weeks since I heard
Gust senior say to Gust junior,
"Ever screw a fat girl?"

IRWIN STREETER:
Worms

"You don't have any bait? No bait?"

We get in the car and take off,
driving deep into the farm country
of northern Illinois.
We watch the signs, all kinds of signs.
Signs everywhere, signs
saying EGGS,
saying RAILROAD CROSSING,
saying NUTRENA FEEDS,
saying KEEP GATE CLOSED,
saying SWEET CORN,
saying ROAD WORK AHEAD,
saying BABY KITTENS,
saying TOMATOES AND BEANS,
saying DO NOT PASS,
saying SPEED LIMIT 55,
saying COUNTY LINE ROAD,
saying FUNK'S G-HYBRID,
saying CUCUMBERS,
saying NARROW BRIDGE,
saying FOR SALE BY OWNER,
saying LEMONADE,
saying BEWARE OF DOG,
saying WATCH FOR CHILDREN,
saying NO HUNTING,
saying DEAD END.
Then, at last, we find it,
a homemade sign nailed to an oak tree
saying WORMS.

"Now, son, you can go fishing again."

PHOEBE YAEGER:
Cheerleader

Feeling
kind of
crazy
this af-
ternoon
before
the big
game with
Central,
I wiped
my face
and knees
with a
monarch
butter-
fly. Now
when I
jump a-
round and
do cart-
wheels, I
sweat our
school col-
ors: orange
and black.
Go team.
Fight team.
Go. Go.
Fight. Fight.

WALTER INGRAM:
In the Middle of the Middle West

Often on hot, humid summer nights,
if I am bored or terribly lonely,
I like to rip up the backcountry roads,
pushing my big blue Buick until she bounces
past corncrib, windmill, and cow barn.
But I also like to just creep along
and look into a lighted farmhouse
where the family is reading the news,
watching television, or playing cards,
or where a boy in a Cubs baseball cap
is tacking a pennant to his bedroom wall,
or where, hopefully, a pretty girl
is walking the kitchen floor in her slip.
It is then I start to glow,
to feel affectionate toward people again.

But this evening I have had too much gin.
The katydids are shrilling in the darkness.
And I am fresh out of love.

The roads, the farms, the good folks
who live on those islands in the corn
will have to wait for that other me.

Damn, it is hard to stay sober here
when one day yawns into the next
and there is little nerve left
to scale the fence, fly the coop.

The Buick sulks under the sullen leaves.

I pass out in my overstuffed chair.

I am being buried half alive
among the tired smiles of used-car salesmen
in the middle of the Middle West.

KIRBY QUACKENBUSH:
September Moon

The old houses, dusted with moonshine,
creak in the dry and dragging wind
that pokes about this town:
where potato salad and cold beans
are eaten in stuffy kitchens;
where, in tubs of tepid water,
ponytailed girls who love fast horses
slide pink soap between their thighs;
where skinny boys lift weights
in bedrooms gaudy with football stars;
where doctors read comic books
and lawyers read numbers on checks;
where sex-starved wives wait in the nude
for tipsy husbands to be bored
with beer glass and cue stick;
where children sleep like stones
and hall clocks tick and tock
and cats yowl and dogs growl,
as another hot Labor Day winds down
in the webbed and wrinkled dark;
and I, moondust on my face,
return from a long walk to the depot,
the depot of many fierce goodbyes;
and it's just this I want to say:
Luanne, my lost and lonely girl,
if you want me on this summer night,
run through the grass now and kiss me.